MIRROR HORSE

TAMARA WILLIAMSON

MIRROR HORSE

Douglas & McIntyre

1   2   3   4   5   —   27   26   25   24   23

Douglas & McIntyre (2013) Ltd.
P.O. Box 219, Madeira Park, BC, VON 2H0
www.douglas-mcintyre.com

Edited by Audrey McClellan
Text design by Carleton Wilson
All photographs by Tamara Williamson except where otherwise noted.
Printed and bound in Canada

Douglas & McIntyre acknowledges the support of the Canada Council for the Arts, the Government of Canada, and the Province of British Columbia through the BC Arts Council.

Library and Archives Canada Cataloguing in Publication

Title: Mirror horse : a memoir / Tamara Williamson.
Names: Williamson, Tamara, author.
Identifiers: Canadiana (print) 20230142117 | Canadiana (ebook) 20230142214 |
    ISBN 9781771623490 (softcover) | ISBN 9781771623506 (EPUB)
Subjects: LCSH: Williamson, Tamara. | LCSH: Horsemen and horsewomen—Canada—
    Biography. | LCSH: Horses—Behavior. | LCSH: Human-animal relationships—Canada. |
    LCSH: Musicians—Canada—Biography. | LCGFT: Autobiographies.
Classification: LCC SF284.52.W55 A3 2023 | DDC 798.2092—dc23

For my late mother

For Aunt Daphne, whose life has opened stable doors
for so many people and ponies

For my son, Angus, who knows how much he means to me

And for all the horses who lived in their own versions of this story.

Mum and Piggy.

Contents

Note from the Author

I wrote this book to open a door into a world that is complicated and nuanced.

A world of horses.

Horses are a great passion for many people. Like other pursuits, they can take you on a journey full of ambition, determination, kindness, frustration, fear and joy. But most passions don't involve another creature, another brain that has its own past, memories, instinct, feelings and character, another animal that has its own big heart.

As a rider you can confuse yourself, thinking you are the teacher or trainer, the brains of the operation, but I think horses are showing us something more important. They are holding up a mirror to our own pasts, memories, feelings, character and, of course, heart.

I had to come out of hiding and find the courage to look in that mirror.

It took a long time.

This book was meant to be about my horses. Instead it took me on a journey I didn't expect and became about more than that.

But I don't want to spoil it.

I hope you enjoy the ride.

Prologue

That moment, that split second when you realize you have absolutely no control. A tiny fragment of time that can stay with you for the rest of your life.

I was fifteen. We were heading home, walking along the bridle path, his neck long and low in front of me, ears pricked. I gathered up the reins and moved him forward into a trot. When we got to the hill, he put weight into the bridle, taking contact. I shortened my reins. Then he made a decision and broke into a canter. I pulled lightly to slow him down, but he didn't respond. I pulled harder, but nothing. A deep, slow panic seeped into my veins as he went faster and faster, like a train. I pulled again. Nothing. Time seemed to be slowing down, and I felt like I was shrinking, turning into a tiny mouse with huge eyes, sitting on his back, watching as the end of the track came rushing toward us. Everything went quiet except for this ferocious movement below me as he flattened out and really started to go. The end of the track meant the road, cars and the bridge over the highway.

I was frozen … it was coming.

I think it was the difference in footing, the clattering of metal shoes on tarmac, that broke the spell and snapped me into action. That's when I pulled frantically on the reins; I was fighting for my life now. I stood up in the stirrups and yanked on the bit with all my might. But he didn't slow at all. So I wrapped the reins around one of my fists and pulled hard with both hands, turning his head until it almost touched my knee. He couldn't see where he was going and he skidded, lurched, took a huge leap and finally stopped.

We stood, his rib cage heaving against my legs.

I could hear my heart thumping.

I was shaking all over.

I waited, summoning the courage to continue back to the yard.

I never told anyone about that day.

CHAPTER 1

Holly, 1976–1978

Tammy, nine years old

Horses fly
They have wings
and flap around my mind
They smile at me
and pick me up
They take me away

The first thing I remember from my childhood is a white horse with a black mane. He was prancing on a pole, part of a merry-go-round printed on the wallpaper in my bedroom. His nose was up in the air and his tail held high; his mouth was wide open, teeth bared and ears flat back. He looked angry, like he definitely didn't want to be on that carousel. The pattern repeated over and over: always the same horse on the same pole looking in the same direction. Except in one corner of my room, high up near the ceiling. There, a single horse lay on his side. No one else noticed him, just me. I would stare and stare at that horse until he came alive. I'd concentrate on him so hard that he would start to move. An ear would twitch and then a hoof would strike the air. I'd push him with my eyes until he righted himself and galloped to the window, where he would jump

Holly getting her treats.

through the open crack and disappear outside. I set that horse free whenever there was enough light to see him, and my heart, for a few minutes, would feel full.

I was born in a stable. My mum gave birth to me in the hayloft. But our stable wasn't in the heart of the English countryside or something poetic like that. It was in the scrubby old town of Putney, in London near the river Thames. Long before I came along, my parents had bought an old riding school, the Kerry Stables, and converted it into a house. It stood on a road of newer flats and council houses but was hidden from view by a tall, red brick wall and large wooden gates. Inside the wall was a cobbled courtyard filled with flower beds, climbing vines, barking dogs, cats, a beehive and a rickety old chicken coop. It made us feel like we had our own secret garden, a magical escape from the busy streets of London.

The Kerry Stables was built in 1853 and was a home for horses until the day before my parents took possession. My father bought the property for four thousand pounds and converted it into an incredible home. The hay racks were still in the corners, attached to the brick walls, with long beams and rafters overhead and split-opening stable doors that looked onto the cobbled courtyard. It gave you the feeling of being in a barn but, with the addition of some huge windows and skylights, was full of natural light. With his flair for design and love of colour, my father made it so much larger than life, and it was somewhat like living on the set of a fabulous movie.

As you entered the house there was a huge kitchen, with bright-red cupboards and a long wooden table, which led to an open-plan sitting room big enough to skateboard around. This "big room," as we called it, had a stage at one end where an apple-green piano sat; comfy blue couches ran along the back wall, with a white fur rug and a swing that we swung on whilst watching the telly. There was a narrow staircase that led up to the hayloft, which had been converted into three bedrooms and a bathroom, all with dramatic sloping rooflines and strange tiny attic spaces for the mice to live in.

The Stables was a wonderful place to live in the summer, cool and breezy, with the half doors always open to the garden, which was shaded by the big old horse chestnut tree. But winter was another story. Due to my father's determination to keep the beauty of the building intact, the Kerry Stables had absolutely no insulation. Sometimes I felt like a character from a Dickens novel, chipping ice off the inside of my bedroom window and sleeping in a woolly hat and gloves because the central heating didn't work and I didn't want to wake up dead. When it rained—and it often rained—the whole house would leak into any number of pots we placed under all the holes. It was often so loud that the dripping would keep us up at night, sounding like a strange orchestra of plopping. My dad was forever up on a ladder trying to mend the roof, but he often only rerouted the leaks and we would have to move the pots over a foot or so. Eventually he gave up and we accepted that this was our lot.

In my memory, my early childhood was filled with wide-eyed wonder and joy. We were a busy, happy, big family. My dad was a self-employed graphic designer, full of stories, plans and elaborate practical jokes. He was well-read, had a huge personality and was funny; it was like living with our own personal Peter Sellers. My mother was jaw-droppingly beautiful, much like Elizabeth Taylor, and was also a fantastic cook. She would make exquisite dishes, like duck à l'orange or beef tenderloin with roasted potatoes dripping in butter. They were a magnetic team and hosted many parties, with their eclectic bunch of friends popping by. Often my brother and I would sit under the kitchen table listening while guests told hilarious stories, talked politics and got into rowdy debates about world economics, religion and love. It was a busy and chaotic daily existence, with a lot of shouting and laughing, and it was never dull. This was the 1970s, with all the fashion and new inventions: flared trousers, platform shoes, my mother's perm, Abba and the exciting day we got our first colour TV. We were living the dream.

England is horse country, so growing up in a huge city like London only boosted my horsey-girl fantasy. There are horses everywhere, or at least that's what it looked like to me. I grew up watching horses pulling carriages for royalty, standing their ground in riots, policing our neighbourhoods and, on the telly, carrying soldiers into battle, pulling cannons and plowing fields. Not to mention the horse sport industries of racing, steeplechase, polo, eventing, show jumping, driving, dressage, carriage racing and, of course, fox hunting. Horses are a large part of the English conversation. I think horse-mad people make up about 30 per cent of the generally eccentric British society, the other 70 per cent being dog-mad people.

Putney was close to both Wimbledon Common and Richmond Park, where many people rode on the numerous bridle paths that are a part of the scenery. It was not uncommon for us to be out walking our dogs and see ten or so horses from the local riding school come trotting past. I always had it in my mind that I would be one of those riders as soon as I was big enough.

I'm not sure if growing up in an old barn was why I was smitten with horses, because none of my stable-born siblings cared about ponies at all. Robbie, my eldest brother, wanted to be a famous explorer; my sister, Lisa, just wanted to eat and stay in her room; and Ben, my closest brother, wanted to play rugby and marry our Cavalier King Charles spaniel. I was the only one who was horse mad. Horses were all I thought about, talked about and dreamed about long before I had even seen one in the flesh, and horses have been my tragic, triumphant, lifelong obsession ever since.

I'm pretty sure some of my horse madness came from my mother. My mum was, as she put it, blue-blooded English aristocracy. Her mother had been a debutante and had tea with the Queen Mother. In fact, both her parents had come from money, but her father, sadly, had been a drinker, gambler and philanderer. During her early childhood he had squandered most of the family's wealth, and they ended up in a small cottage in the countryside near Haywards Heath. My mother rarely talked about her childhood. She was raised in the traditional "children are seen but not heard" English way, but she once told me that she often barked and growled like a dog because as a child she spent most of her time with her pet pug. At the age of eleven she was sent to Saint Mary's boarding school in Wantage, where she was taught by nuns. The only thing she said about this experience was that she didn't mind because she got to take her pony. When she was eighteen, after failing all of her exams, she left boarding school and became a poodle clipper. I think she chose that line of work because her relationships with animals had been the most rewarding and consistent in her life, and she often made reference to the fact that she much preferred dogs to people. She met my father while she was clipping a poodle at a home in Chelsea, when he came in to make a mosaic for the bathroom shower, and three months later they were wed.

My mum was excited when I became besotted with ponies because she knew what it was like to have a burning passion for these animals. She would sit in my room at bedtime and, instead of reading me nursery rhymes, she would tell me about her Exmoor pony named Piggy. There was one particular story that I made her tell me over and over again. Once upon a time, she went out to the field to catch Piggy and found her lying down. At first she thought her pony was sleeping, but then she saw that Piggy couldn't get up. She had broken her leg.

When a horse breaks its leg, recovery is almost impossible because you need to get the weight off the injury to allow it to rest and set. Horses' legs below the knee are very fine and the bones often shatter when they break, so it's hard for them to knit and heal properly. It's also difficult to keep a horse immobile.

The vet arrived and looked at Piggy's leg, then suggested she be put to sleep. My mother was so distraught and cried so much that they decided to try and save her pony. They put Piggy in a sling, hoisting her off the ground to take the weight off her leg, and waited to see if it would mend.

I'd sit transfixed as my mum told me how she would go and feed Piggy treats, hearing her pony nicker as she neared the barn door. When it finally came time to take the sling off, Piggy was so weak that she could barely walk. It took months to build her strength up, but Piggy made a full recovery in the end. My mum would smile and tell me that they never gave up on Piggy, and that she went on to win many prizes and rosettes.

I loved hearing this story and hung on Mum's every word, never wanting it to end. I'd ask for details. Was Piggy in pain? Did she cry? Were you worried the leg might break again? Question after question until Mum would turn off the light and leave the room. I'd lie awake imagining Piggy suspended from the ceiling of the barn, way up high in the rafters, her body trapped in her sling, her legs kicking out, showing her strength as she fought for survival. I'd dream of standing on a tall ladder, holding Piggy's head in my arms and feeding her bright green apples. She would nicker and gaze at me with her big soft eyes as if I were the one she depended on to look after her every need. As if I were her saviour. And my heart would break and mend a hundred times a night.

My own riding life began when I was seven years old. After many hours of my pleading, one day my mother announced she had booked me a riding lesson. From then on, every Saturday morning at eight o'clock we would head out of London and into the countryside to a small town called Claygate, in Surrey. There, nestled in the woods behind a golf course, was a dusty, ramshackle riding stable. It was a friendly place, with chickens and dogs running around and hay bales stacked in every corner. Furry round ponies looked out from each stall door, hoping for carrots and other treats, and it felt like I'd walked into pony heaven.

Going for riding lessons in England was serious stuff. I had to have all the right togs: the mandatory black velvet riding hat, tweed jacket, shirt and tie, cream jodhpurs and polished black riding boots. Before each lesson we groomed our ponies and put oil on their hooves. We'd tack them up and lead them out to a sand ring, where we would follow each other around for thirty minutes while being shouted at constantly by a lady holding a long whip. "Heels down! Shoulders back! Show him who's boss!" Even though I thought it strange that this woman was shouting so much, I didn't mind. I was on a horse and therefore ecstatic. I loved it so much that the first time I went riding I cried for two hours when I got home because it was simply the greatest thing I'd ever done.

I'd plait my hair like a horse, canter around my house like a horse and create jumps in the garden for my horsey self. I'd whinny and paw the ground with my foot, nickering and prancing like a wild stallion. I was for many hours of each day simply... a horse.

After about a year of riding lessons, I got to go on hacks. "Hacking" is another word for riding out on the trails, and to me it was like going on a huge adventure. A bunch of us would go out together, about ten horses in a line, and walk along on a dirt path beside a busy country road. We'd walk for about thirty minutes before we reached a bridle path that ran beside a field. The instructor who was leading the ride would shout something like, "Shorten your reins and hold on," and suddenly we would go full tilt for about one minute up the bridle path. There was no choice in the matter, no other options; we had to hold on to our ponies' manes and go with the others. The horses were happy to follow each other and knew their job, but it was still hair-raising. After our mad gallop we would all turn around and follow our footsteps back to the barn. The ponies would always pick up speed going home, some of them jogging the whole way back. After every ride I would groom my mount, give him a carrot, put him away, get a lift home, polish my boots, hang up my jacket and wait impatiently for the next weekend to arrive.

When I was eight I thought I was ready for my own pony. Everything in my world became a negotiation; I even marked out our garden shed with chalk because I thought it would be best to keep my pony in our garden. I planned out the route to Putney Common, where I could ride each morning, and I decided I could ride my pony to school to save Mum having to drive me. I was relentless in my planning and would bend Mum's ear every day with a new idea on how to carry out my vision.

I'm sure at first my parents must have thought my horse-frenzied behaviour was a passing phase, but as the years rolled by they realized it was not passing anywhere. It must have been lovely for them to see how enthused I was around horses, especially since I was so unhappy at school. Hampered by what my teachers thought to be dyslexia, I found it difficult to keep up and fit in. It was okay at first, but as lessons became more academic I understood less and less. I would sit at the back of the classroom and try to go unnoticed. I simply couldn't understand much of what the teacher was saying. It wasn't sinking in. For instance, learning how to tell the time was torture: I'd stare at the clock, watch the numbers swirl slowly into a nonsensical cluster, and look away in confusion, blotting out anything the teacher was saying. At some point I took to drawing doodles all over my hands and desk. When I got bored of doing that, I'd stare out the window and build my own world. I'd look out onto the netball court and watch as it faded away and turned into a horizon of green fields. Then, as if by magic, there would be reins in my hands and I'd be galloping on a beautiful bay horse, silently, stride by stride in slow motion, like we were floating to the top of that horizon. The sun would fill my eyes, my heart beating faster and faster, and a smile would burst onto my face. The dream was something I could do in class that gave me courage. It was hard on me, not passing any exams and not understanding why, and my dream became the thing that I could count on.

Another thing I took solace in was food. I loved eating. Eating filled me with instant satisfaction, so from the time I was seven I struggled with my weight. My mother put me on diet after diet, and I'd have to weigh myself every day, which added to my neurosis. My being a fatty gave the other kids licence to pick on me; I hated myself for it and ate more to make myself feel better. It was always on my mind; whenever I ate a mouthful of food it was loaded with guilt.

But I don't want to paint a picture of it all being gloomy. I was talented at other things, like singing, and I swam for my borough, but those were extracurricular activities. It was only in the classroom that I couldn't keep up. Every morning became a battle for my parents to get me to assembly; I'd drag my feet, sigh loudly and sometimes pretend to be sick so I didn't have to go at all. My parents didn't pressure me for long; in fact, they seemed to think it was funny. They would pat my head and tell me I was destined for the stage. They had never worried about following rules or fitting in, so why should I? And being rebellious was encouraged in my house. But deep down I cared. I didn't want to be different.

When I was around horses, I felt normal and comfortable. By the age of nine I could name every bone in a horse's leg, every brush in the grooming kit and every part of the saddle and bridle. I was going to become a famous horse-riding star. I was set. I had a goal.

My father was born and raised in Toronto, and he also loved horses. When he was a boy he got a job at the local racing stables, where he would muck stalls and help exercise the Thoroughbreds. He had dreams of becoming a jockey but soon realized how harsh the racing industry was, when his favourite horse disappeared after it lost a few races. He walked away with a broken heart and concentrated his talents on being an artist. In the late 1950s he moved to the South of France, where he worked making mosaics. Picasso commissioned him on several occasions to make his paintings into glass-topped tables. He then moved to London, where he turned his hand to becoming a successful graphic designer.

My dad loved surprises, and it was on my ninth birthday that he strolled in and gave me the surprise of my life. I was sitting watching *Blue Peter* on the telly, and Dad handed me a paper bag with a big ribbon on it. I opened the bag and inside was a carrot. I looked at him, somewhat confused.

"Errrrr, thanks?" I said.

"That carrot," he said slowly, "is for your new pony!"

He literally cheered as he said the pony part. A PONY!

What?

My mouth dropped open and tears rolled down my cheeks. I stood up, not knowing which way to turn. I didn't know what to do with such incredible news. I looked at my dad and asked, "How?"

He explained that he'd heard about a pony called Holly who needed a new mum. She didn't live far away, and we could go there to see her on the weekend.

I couldn't believe it. I gave him a huge hug. I was beside myself with excitement. So I ran into the garden, stood on the climbing frame and sang, "Holly, I love you!" at the top of my lungs, arms stretched out, like I had reached the summit of a mountain. A pony for me? I was in heaven.

That weekend my whole family climbed into our vw camper van and took off for the countryside. About half an hour later we arrived at Barwell Court Farm in Chessington. We parked by a tiny white cottage, and beside that cottage was a small muddy paddock, and in that paddock was a scruffy, shaggy, black-and-white blob of a pony. She was a titchy thing, but she could have had five legs for all I cared. I was so excited and deeply in love.

Holly was about ten hands high, which is about the size of a Great Dane. She was a Shetland pony, a breed originally from

Scotland that was once used throughout Britain, working underground as pit ponies, hauling coal. She was piebald in colour, which means a black horse with large white splashes or patches. I was an average nine-year-old in height, so she was already small for me, but of course I didn't mind. We bought her on the spot for fifty quid, which was probably the equivalent of buying two fancy meals in an okay restaurant. The lady who sold her to us was called Aunt Daphne, and she ran the Sandown Chase Pony Club. Without knowing it, I had landed in horsey-girl heaven, and that one move sealed the next eight years of my equestrian life.

The Pony Club is a network spread across Great Britain and run by volunteers to help produce fine equestrian girls and boys. Joining a branch of the Pony Club was like joining the horse cadet army. It was taken very seriously.

Everything was mapped out for us. At Barwell I was in a group of ten or so girls around my age, all of whom had big personalities and fat ponies, like a Norman Thelwell cartoon. I had found my tribe. My parents were happy because, as it turned out, owning a pony on the outskirts of London was cheaper than riding lessons, and seeing as I was the youngest of four kids, the busier I kept myself the better. We carpooled with the other girls' mums, chatting about our ponies the whole way to and from the farm; it was all such an adventure. We would go to Barwell at 6 a.m. on weekend days and leave late in the afternoon. We'd ride bareback in the fields, groom our ponies, give them baths and braid their manes for hours. We would giggle and make jumps in the woods and just hang around and talk about our four-legged friends all day long.

At last my dream had come true. I had my pony; surely my life was now complete. But it was all quite humbling. As it turned out, Holly was a menace—as most ponies, for some reason, are. In my girlish mind I had this vision of my pony loving me and galloping toward me across green fields, nickering, with loud dramatic music playing in the background. But Holly only put her ears forward for carrots. The rest of the time she was just mean.

On Sunday mornings my new horsey friends and I would go for a hack along the bridle path. We would get about five minutes from the farm when Holly would slam on the brakes, turn and buck me off. Then she'd head for home. *Every time.* I'd pick myself up and trudge back, furious. I'd find her grazing by the gate to her field, looking like butter wouldn't melt.

On Saturday mornings we had riding lessons with an instructor, and I would do maybe one circle in the ring before Holly would put her head right down on the ground and stop. I'd sit there kicking and clicking with my tongue frantically, bright red in the face, but she didn't care; she just stood still, her ears pinned back menacingly. That was how I learned to "use my legs"—a riding term for effective kicks that encourage your mount to go forward.

Holly was as stubborn as could be, and no matter how much stroking, apples and loving I gave to her, she would be hateful when I was riding her. But I refused to give up and kept trying until my feet knocked against her knees and my belly button was as high as her back.

Then one day my mum said to me, "Do you think you need a bigger pony?"

I looked at her, stunned. I don't think the thought had crossed my mind until she said it.

I only had Holly for about eighteen months, but she taught me many things. First, that ponies are naughty. Second, that she didn't care about me much; she just cared about carrots and apples. I still loved her, though—so much. I sold her to another Pony Club girl at a barn in Byfleet, a small village in Surrey. I asked for £150 and couldn't believe it when they said yes. When the horsebox arrived to ship her off, Aunt Daphne loaded her for me. Holly was not pleased about being taken away on her own, and she pawed and whinnied for her pasture buddies. It seemed like such a tragic end. I watched them drive her down the lane, and I could still hear her stamping as they drove around the bend and out of view. It was hard and I was a mess of different emotions, but the biggest was that I felt mean. My dream of having a pony hadn't included selling that pony, and I didn't know how to deal with all those intrusive feelings.

As my eyes teared up, I looked over at Aunt Daphne, who also looked sad. Then she turned on her heel and said, "Come on, Scallywag. Don't worry. She'll be well looked after. Let's go have a cup of tea."

I followed her into the cottage and we moved on to a different topic. I brushed those pesky feelings aside because that's what I was taught to do. You didn't look back; you just looked forward.

And so my life with horses took hold.

Stroller, 1979–1981

Tammy, eleven years old

When I bought my next pony, I had just turned eleven and was deeply entrenched in Aunt Daphne's flock of Pony Club girls. I couldn't wait to get up to the farm every weekend and be in my horsey world. Barwell was about a thirty-minute drive from Putney, up the highway and through the town of Tolworth. It was one of those places where one minute you would be driving through a busy town and the next, with a single turn of the steering wheel, you'd be surrounded by fields.

The Barwell Estate was substantial, with rolling hills, huge pastures, woodland, a lake and cottages scattered over a few hundred acres. The estate was owned by the Barker family. There were two Barker brothers: Tim, who lived on one side of the property in the estate house, and Mark, Daphne's husband, who lived on the other side in Victoria Cottage. Tim Barker was head of the hunt club and had a lovely big yard with about twelve stalls for his horses. As the story goes, Tim didn't want his children learning to ride on his big horses, so he sent them down to Aunt Daphne's yard to learn to ride with their cousins because they had a couple of ponies. One thing led to another, more kids came with more ponies, and over the years Daphne became an aunt to many more pony-loving children.

Stroller ready for cross-country.

Aunt Daphne, as she was known to everybody, was a tall, whimsical woman with that kind of blustery British presence that made you feel like you had stepped into a period novel. She had a striking demeanour, and it looked like her hands and feet were one size too big for her body. She was constantly moving and seemed to swim around the farm, taking care of everyone and everything. She was very kind to all us girls, but at the same time she kept a beady eye on us and shouted at the top of her lungs if something wasn't to her liking. We were all scared of her, which was probably a good thing because it kept us in line. Aunt Daphne knew her horsemanship and was always at hand to help us, in her head scarf, tweed pants, Barbour jacket and Hunter gumboots. She was the head secretary of the Sandown Chase Pony Club. I never saw her on a horse, but she was the boss of my horse world, along with her loyal beagle, Strumpet.

Aunt Daphne and her husband lived in the tiniest of English cottages, with low ceilings and narrow corridors leading off to even tinier bedrooms that looked all wrong when you saw the size of Uncle Mark. He was a huge, hairy man with an enormous bellowing laugh who was always poking fun at us and challenging anything we said. When he was at home, it seemed all he would do was watch rugby and roar with laughter. I loved talking to him and would hang around in their kitchen for hours, chatting away. Uncle Mark and Aunt Daphne had three children, Hugo, Simon, and Annabel, whom we didn't see much of. They went away to boarding school, but when they were home on holidays, they were part of the Pony Club and advanced riders. I looked up to them like they were demigods.

When you looked out the window of Aunt Daphne's cottage, instead of a garden there was a barnyard with about a dozen box stalls and twelve sections for tying horses. The yard was always heaving with ponies and kids of all sizes, coming, going and running around. It took continuous effort to keep it tidy and looking respectable, with its huge flagstones that hid puddles and squelched as you walked along. It was like the whole place was floating on a sea of mud. There were a couple of old caravans that we used as our tack room and also as a kind of clubhouse. We would hang out after riding and play cards for hours, and Aunt Daphne would make us tea with Club biscuits. But most of the time we sat at her table in the cottage and chatted with her about our hopes and dreams. She seemed to love us all, and we all loved her and treated Barwell like our second home.

Although Barwell did feel to me like being in the countryside, it had suffered from "progress," which meant that at some point the A3, a major highway from London to the southwest of England, had landed straight up the middle of the farm. We had to cross an overpass to get to the horses' fields or to go out on hacks, which was a bit scary. Walking your horse on a bridge over a highway was unsettling at the best of times, but there was no choice in the matter. It was there and that was that.

Barwell was home to many horses, about two dozen or more mares and geldings that were kept in separate fields to keep them from fighting. Each field was easily over fifty acres, so the horses had plenty of room to roam. We kept them outside 24/7 because that was the way it was done at Barwell; it also made it more affordable. There was plenty of grass in the spring and summer, and during the colder months Aunt Daphne would feed all the horses every morning and give them plenty of hay. The horses mostly thrived living outside. In fact, some thrived way too much and had to be put on diets.

Catching and bringing in our ponies was a big job. The Racetrack Field, as it was called, where the geldings were kept, was about a fifteen-minute walk from the yard, and it always seemed to be raining or cold. So if someone drove by we would stick our thumb out and jump on their car bonnet or sit in their car trunk with our muddy boots dangling out. Mostly, though, we ended up simply trudging along the laneways. When we finally got to the field, the mud was sometimes so thick by the paddock gate that we would get stuck in it or lose a gumboot. It was like thick, brown glue.

After we had caught our ponies, we would ride bareback home to the yard, with just their head collars on. We would then tie them up, groom them, tack up and go for a ride. We did all this with barely any adult supervision, a whole gaggle of us, and many close friendships were born. There was Lisa Davis on Dundee, Lisa Fox on Pigeon, Sibby Martin on Horace, Kirsty Denny on Merry Legs, Abi Chesover on Trusty and Bryony on Indian, to name a few.

My second pony was excellent. His name was Stroller, which was the name of a famous show jumper ridden by Marion Coakes in the late 1960s. My Stroller was also a super jumper.

Usually, finding a pony happened through the Pony Club or word of mouth, but there had been no ponies around for me to try. Holly had gone, so I was getting itchy to find a new mount. One day Mum and I were in a tack shop, and there on a notice board was a small handwritten For Sale ad for a pony named Stroller. We called the number, asked a few questions and a week later found ourselves driving to Farnham to try him out.

When we arrived, Stroller was standing in a small field with lots of brightly coloured jumps, looking very pleased with himself. The lady who was selling him handed me the reins, looked me in the eye and said, "This pony will never let you down. He is good through and through."

I popped on and rode around for a while, and by the time I got off I was smiling from ear to ear because he was so easy and forward to ride. Stroller was a chunky, compact, handsome gelding, 13.2 hands. His mane and tail were as thick as they could possibly be, and he was very round. We bought him for four hundred pounds, which was a lot of money at the time, but he looked like the perfect fit for me, so my parents found the cash. He was eight years old, which meant he was in his prime, and he was very sure of who he was. We never did figure out exactly what his breeding was, but he was a proper fat British pony, and I was very much in love.

Stroller was also what is known in the horse world as "hot," which meant he had a lot of energy and could be a challenge to control. Thoroughbred racehorses and Arabians are considered hot, but horses can come out hot in any breed. He proved a lot for me to handle after Holly, and for the first year I just hung on most of the time while I rode him. He was a prancer; if he got excited he would start to dance around, which could have been fun if I wasn't so worried. I'd feel the blood start to drain from my face as he would leap and jog.

But as I got to know him, a trust grew between us and we found our connection. Stroller was up for anything and gave me no excuses. In fact, the only job I had was to contain his energy. He taught me how to ride. He was absolutely focused on my every move, so I learned to be a quiet, sensitive rider. I also learned that if I used the correct aids, I got the correct results. When you ride a horse, you need to send them signals with your body so they know what you want them to do. It's a pressure thing, and horses, through riding and training, start to understand a rider's signals, or aids, which become more subtle the further you advance. Developing the skill and timing involved in riding a horse is, in my opinion, much like mastering a musical instrument, except every horse has a slightly different set of strings. Clear signals are vital to get good results from a horse. Learning the aids is the next level up from simply staying on and can take years of practice. Without our realizing it the repetition in our lessons was constantly improving our chops as young horsewomen because our aids became consistent and clear.

One of the best things about having a bigger pony that didn't buck me off was that I could go out together with my friends and explore. The network of bridle paths and woods went on forever behind Barwell, so we would often go out in a gang for the whole afternoon. It was brilliant. We put our lunches in our saddle bags and went weaving our way along the sopping trails up to the woods in Oxshott, mud often above the horse's knees. I fell off a lot. We all did. But we had complete freedom; we did crazy, stupid things, like jumping fallen trees and trespassing through farmers' fields, but we always got back home one way or another. It was all part of the Barwell charm, and it was our place.

My real Pony Club training set in when I got Stroller. Lesson after lesson, circle after circle, we were taught the nuances of being an effective rider. We learned to do smooth upward and downward transitions between the horses' gaits, when to shorten our reins, how to sit trot without stirrups and when to sit as a certain hoof hit the ground. We also learned to jump, and as soon as I soared over my first fence, that was pretty much all I wanted to do.

The Pony Club held rallies once a month so we could be assessed by our instructors. We would dress in our formal show clothes—Pony Club tie, polished boots, jackets and cream jodhpurs—and hack to a field to meet up with other members. We would then have a two-hour lesson. Everything we did was marked, judged and scrutinized: how clean our tack was, how tidy our hair was and how well our ponies were going. All our efforts were aimed at moving up through the different levels of ability, which went from E to A. Each level was represented by a piece of coloured felt attached behind your Pony Club pin, which was worn on the lapel of your jacket. As you moved up the ranks, you proudly swapped in your new felt colour, which showed your riding and horsemanship level. With one quick look you could see if someone was considered further along than you were. It was regimented and structured and, unlike at school, I couldn't wait to take my next exam.

The highlight of our summer was the Barwell Estate horse show, which was run every June. It was a spectacle in every sense of the word. The English love to show off, so everyone would dress in the most country-ish clothes they owned, striding onto the grounds with walking sticks and wearing corduroys and quilted waistcoats, headscarves and flat caps. They would stand around looking proper, usually with a dog of some sort in tow. Then there were the ponies, about a hundred of them, all different breeds and colours, groomed to perfection with their manes and tails braided, and brimming with excitement. They would descend onto the field with all sizes of riders looking very smart, their show numbers tied around their waists and ribbons in the girls' hair. There was a class for everyone, so if your pony didn't jump, you could do the show classes, like fancy dress or best turnout. At the end of the day there were gymkhana classes, which was a crowd favourite: rows of ponies and riders pitted against each other in races like egg and spoon, apple bobbing and bending through poles. We were there from dawn to dusk, and I loved that my whole family would come; my mum would make a huge picnic spread in the back of our VW camper van, and we would spend the day together.

It was clear from early on that I was a competitive child, whereas some kids hated the pressure. Show jumping was my passion, and over the next two years I took to competing with a hunger.

Show jumping is a class that has two rounds. Horse and rider must jump a clear round. If more than one horse and rider "go clear," they go head-to-head in a "jump-off," where you race against the clock. The fastest time with zero knock-downs wins.

Stroller was a fabulous jumper, and because he was hot and fast, we did very well. He could turn and jump anything at almost any angle, so I was soon taking him to larger shows and pitting myself against far bigger horses and older riders. I especially liked being the underdog. We would trot into the ring and nobody would look twice at the podgy girl on the fat little pony. But Stroller had guts and together we had determination. For that one minute in the ring, all my fear would disappear, and I'd just kick and fly. Every competition was to me like the end of a Hollywood movie, where I would finally get the respect I deserved.

I think I yearned to prove myself because I was getting picked on at school and then picked on at home because I was the youngest. It filled me with a burning ambition, but maybe I was also fighting for attention. From as early as I can remember there was a loneliness that followed me around and that I didn't understand.

Riding kept my mind busy with a mixture of excitement and fear, and the adrenaline would also keep me occupied. But sometimes the balance was off, like there was a crow sitting on top of my riding hat that was either with me or against me. The Crow would help me soar over the jumps and grab me when I got off balance; it would help me fly. But some days the Crow would pick me up and fling me to the ground, or peck at my head until I backed off and pulled my horse up. Some days the Crow hated me.

As we went along, the jumps got bigger, up into the three-foot range, which is a big jump on a small pony. But the bigger the jumps got, the better Stroller was. He loved the challenge and would trot into the ring like he owned the world. We won many rosettes and improved at each show, but sometimes he would have an off-day. Eventually we figured out that he hated it when the ground was too slick. He would come out and feel lazy, and I'd get refusals. When a horse goes "behind your leg," it means that they are not going forward with freedom. It's like riding a bike with flat tires. When I got that feeling, there was no choice but to sit back in the saddle and kick him in front of me as best I could—I'd take a deep breath and hope for the best. At that height, if his heart wasn't in it, all of a sudden those jumps looked way bigger, and disaster would strike.

Stroller wasn't being bad; he was being careful, and I was pushing him to risk it all. Over the years we had quite a few messy falls. I broke my nose and my hand at one point, but I didn't dwell on it. That was just part of competing. You had to go for it and sometimes suffer the consequences.

While show jumping was my favourite, the Pony Club was very much into eventing as a discipline. Eventing has three elements—dressage, cross-country and show jumping—which each teach different skills in equitation and produce a well-rounded rider. A day spent eventing was an undertaking, and I was full-on committed to the process. I never overslept or dragged my feet because, for me, going to any kind of event with Stroller was the best day ever. It became another part of our Pony Club lives, and my parents enjoyed spending time chatting with the other parents and eating cucumber sandwiches in the English countryside.

The preparation involved for a day of eventing was considerable. The week before, I'd sit down and memorize my dressage test. Often I would set out an arena in my garden and trot around on foot as though I was riding, learning each turn and circle. The night before, I would go to the barn and ride; give Stroller a bath, scrubbing his two hind white socks; and then take my tack home and clean it with saddle soap, taking every piece of leather apart and shining every buckle. I'd polish my boots and put my show clothes out on my bed, shine my Pony Club badge and brush my helmet with a soft brush. Twelve-year-old me would do all this with no prompting.

The next morning I'd get up at five o'clock, get a lift to the barn, catch Stroller, groom him, then plait his mane and tail using a needle and thread. Aunt Daphne was always there, making sure we were ready and had all the right equipment. She would not tolerate anything but our best. Then about six ponies and riders would walk out into the lane and line up, wait for the horsebox to arrive, load the ponies on, pile in our tack and equipment and drive to the event. When we arrived, we would leave the horses in the box and walk the cross-country course together, then get ready and ride our dressage test from memory in front of a judge. A good dressage result was the easiest way to get into a better position on the scoreboard. It was a simple test at that level. After the dressage test we would take our horse's plaits out, get changed into our special personal colours for the cross-country segment and put the same-coloured bandages on our pony's legs. The cross-country would follow a course of fixed jumps, ditches and banks through the countryside. The whole course was timed so you were meant to go fast; if you didn't finish within the time allowed, you got time faults. The jumps on the cross country course are often referred to as obstacles and some of them have difficulty levels. If you had a refusal, it would cost twenty points; if you fell off, you were eliminated. After the cross-country we would change back into our tweed jackets and ties and do the show-jumping segment. Unlike show jumping generally, this was only one round of jumps. If you had a knock-down or refusal, you would get another twenty points added to your dressage and cross-country score. Often the most well-rounded equestrian would win the day, and that's what the Pony Club encouraged.

When we weren't riding, we would be in our gang eating fried egg sandwiches and too many sweets, and watching each other's rides. We would also hand-graze our ponies for hours, listening to the loudspeakers announcing how our friends were doing. Pony Club against Pony Club.

Finally we would all go and check our scores, get our rosettes, then put the ponies in the horsebox and return to Barwell. After we got back to the barn, we would groom them and put them in their fields, then get a lift back into London from one of the mums. And that was our day, an exciting, challenging and stupendously exhausting day.

Stroller and I didn't do very well at eventing, which was mostly because of me. The cross-country frightened me: the fences were far apart and that gave me way too much time to get nervous. I didn't like the speed, and I'd often be shaking with fear at the start gate. I was mostly worried about crashing into a fence. There are two trains of thought when it comes to jumping and finding your distance. Some people believe the horse should find his own stride and adjust himself if he is too close or too far away from a fence. In the Pony Club, though, we were taught to help our horse by seeing the correct stride. But when you are galloping fast toward a cross-country fence, it's hard to see the distance, and if your horse gets it wrong, you might have a spill. The cross-country fences are fixed, which means the rails don't fall when you hit them. This means getting the distance wrong has the potential to cause a nasty crash. I saw many people tumble off and go flying into wooden rails at high speed. I was too cautious; I'd slow down before each fence and canter into it, and therefore take too long and get time faults. Some of my friends loved cross-country and hankered to gallop, but I had to make myself do it because I wanted to be part of the occasion. I swallowed my fear because we didn't show fear—ever. Fear was for wimps. Stroller, on the other hand, thought everything was fun and picked up his knees over every jump I pointed him at. He loved the challenge and carried me around.

Brave
His heart bigger than my head
Eyes forward
One foot in front of the other
Magnificent
My round friend

Stroller, a stride early in the jump-off.

Competing and having goals became part of my life. I was always on my way to the next show, with a new adventure coming over the horizon. My parents were very supportive and got swept along with my dreams, to the point that my dad bought a horse trailer. This cut down on expenses because the horsebox rental for each show was very costly. He shopped around and ended up ordering a small two-horse steel trailer, which he had sprayed the same pea green colour as our vw camper. It was, well, very... striking. From then on, he became the one who took me to most of the shows because my mum hated driving with the trailer. I didn't mind because it meant I got to spend more time with my dad. But it may have been one reason why my mum became less involved in my life.

The Pony Club also got us to take part in tetrathlon, which is a multidiscipline event where participants compete in shooting, swimming, riding and running. It was an honour to be asked to represent Sandown Chase, and when they called and asked me to be on the team, my mum and dad were both thrilled. I had to train hard, but I was a strong swimmer and turned out to be an okay shot, and with Stroller to back me up on the cross-country, it looked like I would be a contender. My dad thought it was hilarious and took many pictures of me holding a pistol, looking menacing. I did okay at tetrathlon, but the thing that let me down was my running. I found running impossible; there was no bounce in my step at all. It was probably because I was overweight, like I was carrying a slab of concrete on my back. I remember one event where I had to run a mile, and I gave up and walked it. With a huge amount of shame and sadness, I watched other girls sprint past me. I didn't want to be the fat kid, but I couldn't stop eating, especially toast and butter. As soon as my mum would leave the house, I'd shove down as many slices as I could and feel like a loser. I'd gain weight until the zip wouldn't go up on my jodhpurs and then go on some extreme diet or other, lose ten pounds and then, over the next two weeks, gain it all back again. My mother was absolutely relentless with my dieting, so I was constantly thinking about food. My weight loss and gain became cyclical, and I couldn't look in the mirror without sucking in my cheeks, pulling in my stomach and, all in all, feeling bad about myself.

I bought Stroller in my final year of Roehampton Church School, which was a good school for me outside of the classroom. It was on the side of Putney Common, where we could run around on lunch breaks and play ponies. It was a small school, which I liked, and only had about thirty children in each year. Although my grades were bad and I struggled, I made some good friends. My favourite and best friend from the age of three was Lisa Davis. We understood each other in some unfathomable way and spent most of our time together. She was very smart and at the same time very funny, and we would play in our imaginary pony world every lunch break. Lisa loved riding as much as I did, so it wasn't long before she joined the Barwell clan.

Roehampton Church School had a legendary music program—choir and orchestra—and put together elaborate school plays. By this time I was getting quite the reputation as a singer, as my mother had sent me to private voice lessons. Singing was always natural for me; I took exams, advanced up the classical singing levels with not much effort and enjoyed being a soprano in the church choir. I was also interested in the art classes and loved painting and drawing with ballpoint pen, so as much as I hated going to school, I have some fond memories too.

During that final year at Roehampton Church, we had to take exams that would determine where we went for secondary school. The exams were hard, and there was a lot of pressure. My teachers and my parents were worried about where I would end up with my low grades. I didn't want to go to comprehensive school, where it was rumoured kids regularly got beat up. So every day after the bell rang I would stay behind and get extra instruction. This helped me retain, by memory, answers to many questions that might come up in exams, but I still didn't understand the concept of learning, so it also strengthened my feelings of inadequacy. It was as if I was being schooled in the art of exam passing, like we were tricking the system. I knew it was important and could change my future, so I put my head down and tried hard not to disappoint anyone.

After hours and hours of tutoring I managed to get into a very academic, private, all-girls school called Putney High. It was strict, with lots of rules. We had to wear purple-and-grey tunics and behave like fine young ladies. We learned to sew and cook, and played netball and rounders. I knew by the end of the first day that I was out of my league and I wasn't going to keep up. It was English and proper and an environment that made me want to rebel. So over the next five years I went from being a fairly-happy-sometimes kid to being a very-unhappy-most-of-the-time teenager. I sat at the back of the class and disappeared, not even bothering to try to be funny anymore. No one there cared or understood anything about my riding dream, and the school barely had any music or a decent art program. It was a bad fit.

My home life was also taking a nosedive. My mother had always liked the odd drink, but as I grew older her drinking took over. I didn't know what was going on; I only knew she had a lot of headaches and wasn't as interested in my life as she used to be. My dad was getting more and more irritable, and my days faded in front of my eyes, losing their colour. My pony and my goals as a rider became the only things in my life that I looked forward to. Barwell became my second home, and Aunt Daphne became a parent figure to me, someone I could rely on.

I had Stroller for three summers, but as time ticked by I got taller and he seemed to get smaller. At the end of our third show season together, I decided we had maxed out our potential as a team and it was time for me to get a bigger pony.

Our last summer showing together was when Stroller and I hit our stride. The biggest memory I have was when I jumped him over four feet at a "Chase Me Charlie" event at our local show. This is a gymkhana class where you see which horse can jump the highest by putting the fence up a hole every round. He beat all the other horses that had entered that day, and I mean horses. Remember, he was only 13.2 hands, which is considered a mid-size pony. The whole showground was watching because it was the last event of the day. Twenty horses were lined up. Some of the small ponies made it to about two-foot-nine. Then the next bunch had rails down at about three-foot-six, but we kept going. In the end it was a contest between me and this other girl, and the jump kept going up. At four-foot-one she took the rail down. It was my turn and Stroller was excited. Everyone went quiet as I tried to aim this wildly bouncing pony at the fence, then three-two-one strides and—pop. He jumped right over, like it was nothing. Everyone cheered. I collapsed on his neck laughing. The fence was huge; we were literally looking up at it.

My perfect bay pony.

He never let me down.

I sold Stroller to a family with three young Pony Club daughters a long way away so I wouldn't be able to see him unless I arranged a visit. I did this because I didn't want to watch someone else ride him, but I also knew this meant that I would have to say goodbye. My mum and dad also loved Stroller. They had watched me grow up from eleven to almost fourteen on this pony, and he represented a huge amount to all of us. It must have been difficult for them to see him go, but we couldn't afford to keep two horses.

When the day arrived to take him to his new home, my mum didn't want to come. She told me that she couldn't bear it; it was one of the only times I ever saw her be openly emotional. So my dad and I took him in the trailer. I wanted everyone there, the whole family. But we didn't do things together anymore, and nobody insisted. When we arrived at his new home, we showed Stroller around and gave him some apples, and then it was time to say goodbye. It was a tough moment because there were so many people around, and I didn't know what to say. We didn't show emotion in front of each other in our family—or in England for that matter—so I gave Stroller a pat and said, "Good boy."

I wanted to tell the new owners as much as I could about him before I left, important things like how he enjoyed apples more than carrots. That you had to make sure he didn't eat too much fresh grass. That he didn't like being at the rear on trail rides, and that he was the best pony in the world. I knew it was a good home for him, but it was hard to hand over the reins. We all stood around Stroller and a silence set in, so I nervously made a few jokes about him being fat and his mane being too thick to plait. Everyone laughed and we shook hands and I walked away feeling bad about myself.

Stroller had saved that part of my childhood. Without him I would have been the chubby, dumb kid at the back of class, but with him I was a winner. He brought out the best in me as I rose to the challenge of keeping up with such a clever, courageous pony. I couldn't look him in the eye when I said goodbye because he was too important.

I was very lucky to have had him.

Cut
Cut the friendship
Cut the tie
Cut out feelings
Don't look back
Don't pay homage
Just cut
And move forward

Stroller lived until the end of his days with the same family and was truly loved. Twenty-one years later, my mother phoned me and told me his owners had called to say he had died of old age. He was out in the pasture and lay down and didn't get up. As my mother was telling me, I burst into tears and cried like a baby. Or maybe like a thirteen-year-old girl should have cried when she said good-bye to the pony she loved. It was a spontaneous and immediate response to the news, and it came from a hidden part of my being that had not said goodbye at the time. Being told to be tough and suck it up can have its consequences, and I don't think in my child-hood I was ever told that it was okay to feel and to love. At the age of thirteen I was already good at stuffing emotions, like clothing, into cupboards deep down in my ribs. I didn't even bother to fold them first.

So maybe I'll take this opportunity to say:

Thank you, Stroller. I love you. And goodbye.

CHAPTER 3

Woofy, 1981–1983

Tammy, thirteen years old

Whirling mane
wandering eye
hot rain
black sky
rears astride
away now
hit hide
rider scowl
horse falls
rider screams
horse dies
all a dream

(A two-word poem I wrote at Putney High in 1982.)

The day we dropped Stroller off, his new owner told me on our way back to the car that there was a horse for sale next door that I might like. I smiled and pleadingly gazed at my dad.

"We might as well take a look, since we're here anyway," he said, with an air of excitement.

Woofy showing her remarkable beauty.

We knocked on the door of the neighbours' cottage, and the owners came out and said yes, they had a mare for sale. They had had her for a year but their daughter had given up riding. They added she was green broke, which usually means a horse has been given about thirty days of training.

Grazing happily in a large field beside the cottage was a pretty, dapple-grey pony. She was a Welsh cob and Arabian cross, about 14.2 hands high.

Arabian horses have been around for thousands of years and tend to be fine boned and hot. They were actually bred to be war horses and are incredibly fast, strong and powerful. Because they originated in the Arabian desert, they are also tough and make very competitive long-distance horses in modern endurance racing. Arabians have what is called a dished face, a concave profile that is a signature of the breed. The Welsh cob, on the other hand, is synonymous with the English countryside. These ponies are hardy, strong and good competitors. This was a good combination of breeds and could lead to a potentially nice competition horse.

The mare looked very pretty from the fence and was a nice type, with a medium build and good conformation. As we got closer, we saw that she was filthy: her mane and fetlocks were thick with burrs, and she looked like she had not seen a brush for a few months. I thought to myself, "I should save this pony and give her the home she deserves." I didn't stop to think that a grey horse always looks dirty in muddy old England, and burrs are just burrs that you brush out. I had £800 in my pocket from selling Stroller, and they only wanted £250 for her because she hadn't done much. It appeared to be perfect, like fate had swept down and dropped this pony into my lap. I talked to my dad, who was maybe too in love with spontaneity, and we bought her—like buying a pair of nice new shoes without even trying them on first. No thinking it through, no ensuring that it was the right fit. I didn't even ride her. We bought her and put her straight onto the trailer. Or at least we tried to. She didn't think the trailer looked like a good idea at all, and it took a lot of convincing to load her.

Her name was Mary Malinda but I called her Woofy. I was going to train her to be a superstar jumper. The problem with this plan was that I forgot to ask Woofy if that was what she wanted. At eight years old she was in her prime, but she had basically stood in a field being a glorified lawn mower until that point.

I had just turned thirteen and I thought I was good enough to train a pony. I wanted to show Woofy the next summer, so it was game on. When I got her back to Barwell, she allowed me to get on her, which was good because we didn't even know how long it had been since she had been ridden. I set about schooling her in the basics. I had a lot of help from the Pony Club, and we had regular lessons, so it went well, but that was partly because she was fairly compliant at the beginning. She learned walk, trot and canter easily, and my instructor was happy with her, but I didn't like the feeling she gave me. I put it down to the fact that she was learning, but she felt flat and bored.

It was when we got to jumping that her lacklustre approach became obvious. She showed absolutely no interest. This was a big letdown because jumping was what I wanted to do. She looked the part of a jumping superstar: I cleaned her up, pulled her mane, trimmed her fetlocks and got her into shape, and she was stunning. But riding her was like riding a dairy cow. We entered the odd show and got around the course, but it was nothing like the feeling I'd had on Stroller. I tried feeding her a bucket of oats before shows to give her energy, but it did nothing. She found it all boring. I wasn't used to boring, and this was not the fairy tale that I had sold myself.

The other problem was getting her to shows in the first place: she grew worse and worse about getting on the trailer. We tried everything. We put the trailer in her field and fed her on it every day, which helped with loading her as long as the trailer was in the field. As soon as it was attached to a vehicle, she would look at me as if to say, "I'm not stupid, you know," and she'd dig in her heels and flatly refuse to load.

I'd get her all bathed, because when you have a grey pony you must bathe them all the time, and plait her beautiful soft white mane. She would be ready in her shipping boots, looking fabulous. Dad would drive up and I'd lead her out of the yard, but as soon as she saw the trailer she would stop. Sometimes it took an hour or two before we would get her on board. Once, she lay down on the ramp—just slowly sank to the ground. That was her trick: not fighting. We would offer her carrots, then grain, and then put a lunge line around her bum and try to pull her in. Throw a bucket of cold water at her back end. Make loud sounds behind her. We even tried riding her into the trailer, which is dangerous and not very Pony Club, but no, she just stood there not moving. And honestly, it was like a betrayal. After all my effort, after I'd saved her, why did she hate me so?

When and if I got her to the show, she didn't like any of it. We would only do okay. Then I'd have to put her back on the trailer, and the ordeal would repeat itself, only with spectators.

When you are at a horse show and your horse won't load, you must deal with all the horse-trailering "experts" coming out of the woodwork to lend a friendly helping hand. They often say clever things like "Trailering is training. You should take her home and do more groundwork." Or "You need a bigger trailer." Or "She's taking advantage of you." It was always the horsey-girl mothers who had a lot to say; the fathers would stand around watching with their arms folded, except for the occasional man who thought he was stronger than a horse. I once had four men try to lift her up the ramp; at least that was funny.

This was my first taste of righteous outspoken horsewoman syndrome. Like mothers who ask other mothers if their babies sleep through the night, it was judgy and passive-aggressive. My mum was very proper, with a sharp wit and a way of dropping a comment that would hush a whole room. If someone said, "I don't mind if I do," she would quickly quip, "Well, if you don't mind, don't." In a situation like this, she would look at us, one eyebrow very slightly raised, and we would all crumple with laughter. But when Woofy took to standing on the ramp of the trailer at horse shows, even my mum took to sitting in the car and ignoring the whole saga. It was dreadful.

By this time my home life was unravelling into a thousand strands of crazy. My father was a creative, artistic and charismatic man, but he had a wandering eye. He was the life and soul of our house, and I always loved it when he came home from work. But he was coming home later and later. Sometimes he didn't come home at all. My mum was drinking more and more, and they would have huge fights, which sometimes involved throwing things. We all began walking on eggshells around each other.

My siblings were growing up and leaving the nest. My eldest brother, Robbie, went to explore the world on a tall ship with a group called Operation Drake. My sister, Lisa, went from being a typical angry teenager to being one of the first punk rockers in London. It was shocking and caused more fighting in the house as she got the confidence to tell my parents what she thought to their faces. She would bring home crazy-looking boyfriends with safety pins through their noses and tight stripey pants covered in zips. My other brother, Ben, became a kind of academic recluse; he pretty much lived in his room, studying. I took a liking to bunking off school, hiding from my parents, going to parties and finding out about boys. Suddenly my family was never around the same table, and we all acted like it didn't matter.

School became a juggle between how often I actually went and how often I could get away with bunking off. I'd take the odd stab at trying to understand, but every time I did I'd get no reward. My brain just could not retain the information set in front of me. I also didn't fit in socially at Putney High: the beautiful, tall, slim, clever girls would all hang out together, and I hated them from a distance. At the same time, I wanted desperately to be included.

Then one glorious day in the second year, I was walking down the stairs at Putney High and saw Lisa Davies standing at the bottom with a big grin on her face. I was over the moon. Lisa had been my best friend all through primary school and, better still, was my Barwell buddy. Her parents had bought her a pony called Dundee who looked exactly like Stroller, and we rode together all the time. When I got Woofy, Lisa bought a lovely bigger pony called Beth and, side by side, we continued on our Pony Club journey together. Lisa had also hated her new secondary school and talked her parents into switching her to Putney High so we could be together. Until that point I didn't have any close school friends, and I remember being so relieved to see her. We became inseparable. We were the same height and build, so we even looked alike. We wore our long brown hair in the same style, and we both had black pointy flat shoes that we thought were incredibly cool. We adapted the boring purple Putney High uniform as much as we could without getting detentions, and walked the corridors on the right side instead of the left, which was the *rule*. We were rebellious and outsiders together and I loved it. The only annoying thing about our relationship was that she did exactly the same amount of concentrating in class as I did but always got an A. It was confounding. But when Lisa came to Putney High, my life improved one hell of a lot.

Pony Club camp took place every summer in Cobham, a small town in Surrey. About sixty horsey girls and maybe one boy camped together with their ponies for a week. In spite of the militaristic feel, which of course kept us in line, we couldn't wait for camp and wouldn't have missed it for the world.

Camp was held on a vacant farm in a harvested straw field beside a graveyard. The farm stood at the edge of a town, like a vestige of a time gone by, and looked to be trying with all its might not to get eaten up by the subdivisions that were marching toward it. The straw field sloped away to surrounding green pastures and hedgerows and was about ten acres in size. There were various dusty outbuildings that we put to good use: the pig barn acted as the latrine, the hay barn was the mess hall and the grain shed became our tack room. For the old farm, camp must have been like putting paddles on a dead man and seeing the life flood back into his veins. It was suddenly a hive of activity and drenched in colour as we divided it into separate areas, one full of show jumps, another with dressage rings, and a space for gymkhana games. Camp was held in the middle of our school holidays, right after the farmer had gotten one cut of straw off the field. So for the whole of our week we would not walk around; we would swish around, navigating the lines of yellow stubble that gave the field a golden glow.

Cobham was about a twenty-minute drive from Barwell with the horse trailer, but what we loved doing most was hacking to camp. A group of us would leave Barwell together and navigate the trail systems up through Oxshott, with a map in our pocket in case we got lost. We could get almost the whole way on bridle paths, part of the fantastic network of trails running through the British countryside. It was about a two-hour journey on horseback, and I always felt a bit like a cowboy setting out on a big adventure.

As we arrived we were split into four teams, and for the entirety of camp we would live, breathe and eat being the best team. It was very much like boot camp; there were older kid leaders who were like sergeant majors, some of whom were nice and some of whom were not. We didn't have to salute them, but we did stand to attention and did everything we were told.

The ponies were kept in long rows of temporary box stalls, in sections for each team. Our sleeping accommodations were also in sections near the barns and consisted of old caravans and an array of colourful tents, but I was one of the luckiest because I got to use our vw camper van." The parents, who volunteered, did a spectacular job of keeping the whole thing running smoothly and feeding us all from vast metal troughs of full-force hearty British food. This included a full English breakfast with scrambled eggs and bacon every morning.

Our daily routine began at 6 a.m. with feeding the ponies and giving them hay. We would then diligently muck out the stalls. We got marks for everything we did, and the marks were put on the scoreboard each night. Because we were so competitive and wanted to win, mucking our stalls would take an inordinate amount of time. We would make the straw banks have corners, which required ridiculous amounts of plumping and patting down. We would scrub out our water buckets and stuff our hay nets in an organized manner. All before breakfast. The cleanliness scorekeeping extended to our tents, where points for daily spot checks went toward team marks. We were also marked on our turnout, which meant our tack was inspected and we were checked to be sure that we had our hairnets, gloves, jackets and ties on, and that our boots were polished at every lesson.

We rode our horses twice a day for two hours each session: dressage in the morning and show jumping in the afternoon, or sometimes cross-country jumping through the surrounding fields. The best, and most loved, afternoon lesson was taking the horses swimming. About ten of us would get in our swimsuits and ride bareback down to the river. Some horses would love it and would immediately jump into the water and start pawing and splashing all of us until we were dripping wet. Other horses, including Woofy, would stand at the bank and refuse to even put a toe in. So we would take turns on the agreeable ponies, riding them into the deep part of the river until they started to tiptoe as they got out of their depth and swam. It was like sitting on a seahorse. Their back ends would drop right down as they paddled frantically with each front leg or lunged ahead in a huge leaping movement. We would lean forward, clinging to the mane for as long as we could while the deep, dark water lapped around our waists and we slipped about on their sopping backs. My face would ache from smiling as we walked back up to the campground, clean, tired and happy.

After a full day with the horses, we would say goodnight to them and then play games in the field until dusk or sit in lectures about conformation or gauging a horse's age by looking at their teeth. We would clean our tack until the leather was soft and supple and every metal buckle shone, and then go to bed exhausted.

Of course, it wasn't all perfect. I have nothing but good memories from the early years of camp, but as we got older it became more competitive and weighted. And putting sixty girls together for a week meant there were bound to be some rivalries. There was even one incident where a scuffle broke out and Aunt Daphne tore through the tents, finding two girls at each other's throats. Unfortunately, when she came upon them she tripped on a tent peg and ended up with an enormous black eye, which caused the girls oodles of guilt as they watched her bruise turn many shades of purple and yellow as the week wore on.

Luckily, I shared the camper van with Lisa Davies, and we nearly always got along. I also became good friends with another Lisa, Lisa Fox, who got me into tons of trouble. She was like the perfect cute button everyone wanted on their jacket. Big dark eyes and turned-up nose, and she was naughty. I liked her. We decided, on discussion, that instead of winning fairly, maybe sabotage would be in order, and I remember we all got pretty good at flicking hoof oil at the other girls' cream jodhpurs. We would also tear holes in each other's hairnets. And when it was time to muck the stalls, all of the forks and shovels would disappear from the other teams' stables.

Lights were turned out at 9 p.m., which led to more adventures—like sneaking out late at night to the graveyard in our pyjamas to tell ghost stories. We would signal across the campground with our torches, hide behind gravestones and pounce on each other in the pitch-black night. When we were about fourteen, some of us snuck alcohol into camp, gathering in someone's tent to swig our mothers' vodka and feel enormously proud of ourselves. These were the days of the *St. Trinian's* films about rebellious school girls and the *Carry On* films about rebellious adults, and I think we believed that part of being British was being naughty and having a laugh. We saw breaking the rules as honourable.

I was eleven when I first went to camp and went every year until the maximum age of sixteen. But during those years I noticed that when Pony Clubbers hit their teens, the numbers started thinning out. Those of us who were left looked after the younger ones and became leaders. This was a big responsibility and we were sometimes horrible to them; they probably walked away scarred for life. If they were lippy, I'd make them clean my tack, muck my stall and scrub my water buckets. It was like an overlord situation where, honestly, it was all a tad abusive, but that's what we were used to. If you showed emotion, you were told to toughen up and were given more work to do. I'd feel bad about it, but then I'd recall all the times I'd been picked on when I was a younger horsey girl. I'd say, "Lucy, I think I saw your pony running around loose in the straw field," and watch Lucy scream and run toward the stables. We would roar with laughter and congratulate ourselves on being so mean. I do remember some nice moments of camaraderie, though not that many, and no place was as evil as standing by the scoreboard, a huge white board with everyone's individual marks and team rankings. If someone in your group was letting the team down, you could either help them or pick on them mercilessly. Most of the time we did both. All in all, though, we did work together, and we did have a fun time.

Occasionally things went a little haywire, and one of the most legendary events was the trifle war. Our parents were all big volunteers because there was always lots to do at camp. The dads would do manly things like helping to get the grounds ready, and the mums would clean the latrines and help with the never-ending mountain of food that needed to be prepared. Mostly we ate quite simple meals, but as the years progressed the mums began to get as competitive as their daughters and were constantly trying to outdo each other and serve us the most memorable dishes possible. Lisa Fox's mum was one of my favourites. She wasn't like a parent at all; she was more like one of us. At one camp she decided to make a large trifle. Enough for sixty, which is a stupendous thing to do. She had good intentions but, sadly, her pudding plan hadn't factored in the transport time, with car heat and jiggling, so the trifle arrived on our plates in a much-diminished form. One of the girls, refusing to eat it, returned it to Lisa's mum and explained, while waving her fork full of trifle in the air, that it was soggy. As she did this, a large piece of trifle flew off her fork and hit Lisa's mum, who then took a huge spoonful of the topping and shot it straight back at the girl, hitting her squarely in the face. There was a moment of stillness and then all hell broke loose as a huge trifle food fight broke out. Sixty girls screamed in delight as pudding was flung around in a moment of pure abandon. Trifle was dripping from the rafters, clinging to every surface and stuck in our hair. Our jodhpurs were also sticky and covered in pink and yellow stains until camp ended. Aunt Daphne was not amused. We spent many hours cleaning it up, but we were all grinning as we wiped each chair and table down.

Camp culminated on the last day with a big eventing competition. All the parents came and watched. By then we would be

Pony Club camp prize ceremony.

exhausted and filthy, as there were no showers. We would walk our parents around the grounds and show them everything we had achieved, with our breeches covered in hoof oil, sweat and sand. Then we would attend the final prize-giving ceremony on our ponies and in full regalia. The best team would be awarded the camp cup, with ribbons for each team member, by the district commissioner of the Pony Club, Sue Challis. Individual prizes were handed out for things like best turnout mark for the whole week or best mark for tidiest tent. There would be some speeches and lots of laughter as Aunt Daphne would talk about some high and low points of the week's adventure. After that we would pack up our stuff and put the ponies on a horse box or trailer, too exhausted to ride home, and wave goodbye to our friends and camp for another year.

Woofy did okay during camp week. I had to concentrate on dressage because her jumping ability was not worth focusing on. In the end I finally found her a job when we realized that she loved standing still. It doesn't seem like an asset in a horse but, as it turned out, I could do anything to her—stand on her back, train kids to vault on her, sit under her tummy—and she didn't care. We used her at camp for braiding lectures, grooming lectures and points-of-the-horse lectures, and she stood still for hours.

When I got home I entered her in our local shows in a class called Family Pony. This is where you show how bombproof your horse is and how suitable for any member of the family to ride. I'd go in and crawl around her legs and all over her, swing off her neck and leapfrog off her hind end, and she would stand there stock-still, not even trying to eat grass. Because of her considerable beauty, we won many rosettes and ended up being awarded Family Pony of the Year at the local Barwell show. This led to qualifying for the major show circuit, and that's when I saw the opportunity to sell her. I wanted out. I did not like showing classes because they pitted horses against each other based on their looks, and riders on who wore the nicest jacket. I wanted to jump again and prove myself with a clear round. Now that Woofy was a champion, I could get enough money from selling her to buy myself a jumper. I advertised and found her a new home at a show barn. When I told the new owners that she was bad at getting on the trailer, they looked at me like it was my fault because I obviously wasn't doing it right. I smiled sweetly, handed them her lead rope and walked away. Apparently it took them a while to get her up the ramp.

Woofy was formidable in a lot of ways. She showed me that she had a strong sense of who she was, and she was not going to change for anyone. She was happy not doing much, and she hadn't wanted to be saved. I was frustrated with her, but one thing she didn't do was scare me, which was like a holiday from my nerves.

I thought I was going to create a masterpiece when I found her. I thought that buying a horse with no past record and training her to be a prize-winning jumper was somehow going to prove my worth as a rider. That this didn't happen had as much, or more, to do with the fact that I was dealing with a living, breathing creature as it did with my ability. I could have spun it differently and congratulated myself on bringing her along and winning the Family Pony classes. But I was hard on myself, and with my so-called failure came a loss of confidence in my abilities.

If I had slowed down that day when I first met her, I might have seen that she wasn't the right horse for me. I could have put her on a lunge line and popped her over a few jumps, and even my thirteen-year-old self would have noticed that she showed no interest. Had I been wiser, I would have thought about the stupidity of buying an eight-year-old lawn ornament in the first place. Instead, I went for my dream, and when she didn't fulfill my hopes I felt robbed. I blamed her and her stubborn nature for letting me down. I came to the conclusion it wasn't my fault. I had done everything right and worked hard. But the truth was that I had thrown my heart into the air and asked fate to make me a hero.

Where was my reward for being so romantic?

For having big dreams?

Where?

Woofy went on to become a good broodmare.

I'm sure that's all she wanted to do.

That and stand still.

CHAPTER 4

Barnaby Rudge, 1983–1987

Tammy, fifteen years old

No No No
I'm up here
Stop
Don't
Whoa
It's blown
I'm gone
Sheer
Panic
Pull
Pull
Pull

There were a lot of horses and ponies at Barwell, and none of them were perfect. Many of my friends had problem horses: some were spooky, some would buck when they got excited, some were hard to catch and some reared, which was incredibly dangerous. One of the Barwell girls had been severely injured when her horse reared up, flipped over backward and landed on her, crushing both sides of her pelvis. She spent a long time on crutches.

49

Barnaby.

As we got into our mid-teens, the reality that these creatures could be dangerous was setting in. The more we learned, and the bigger the jumps got, the higher the stakes became. We never talked about a "bolter"—a horse that runs away with its rider—because we all galloped around so much that we thought all our horses were bolting off all the time. But there is a difference: a horse that actually bolts is fairly rare and very dangerous.

Stroller had set the bar high for me because he had no "vices"—a term horse people use for serious behaviour issues. I had wasted two summers on Woofy, but now I had a chance to put things right and do well. I strode on into my future, thinking I should find another, bigger Stroller, but I wanted a lighter horse this time. I wanted a Thoroughbred cross that would be a good all-round competition horse, and this time I wanted another gelding. After my two mares, Holly and Woofy, who were very opinionated and strong-willed, I craved the stable temperament of a gelding like Stroller.

Abi Chesover on Trusty (left), Lisa Fox on Boy, and me (front).

Geldings and mares are different in more ways than gender. A good mare can be an excellent horse to ride, but when they go into season, life can get complicated. A difficult mare can be witchy, temperamental and stubborn. Geldings have the reputation of being easier, but some people think they can be a little bland. It seems there are two kinds of people: people who like mares—and smart people. 😊 Then there are stallions, which are male horses that aren't gelded. Stallions can be harder to handle and were uncommon in the Pony Club. Like male dogs that aren't fixed, they can have a one-track mind around mares and get overexcited. You get the odd one that doesn't know he's a stallion, but mostly we were discouraged from going near them.

There were many horses at Barwell that had some Thoroughbred in their family tree, mainly because of the massive horse-racing industry in England. There are tons of historic racetracks and prestigious events, like Cheltenham Racecourse, the Grand National Steeplechase at Aintree, Royal Ascot at Ascot Racecourse, and the Epsom Derby at Epsom Downs. A day at the races gives Brits a chance to hold on to some long-standing traditions, and if you attend a race meeting, you will notice that almost everyone wears a hat and seems charming. You will likely also see a member of the Royal Family watching from the royal box at the larger events.

Because of the size of this industry and the wealth involved, there are many studs scattered across the British Isles that produce Thoroughbreds. These horses are painstakingly bred to be fast, hot, quick-switched racing machines that can reach speeds of over forty-five miles per hour. Racehorses tend to be brought up in a quick-learning environment and sometimes have behavioural and health issues because they are pushed to run races when they are still as young as two years old. Many horses break down, which usually means they have leg injuries, some of which are fatal, and some horses retire from racing because they don't run fast enough.

Consequently, there were always a lot of "off-the-track" Thoroughbreds looking for homes, though they tended to be too hot and hard to handle for us Pony Club kids. If you could find a three-quarter Thoroughbred, maybe with some cob or Welsh pony blood in the parentage, then you had some hardiness and a cooler horse spirit. It was a good mix.

By this time I thought that eventing would be the better equestrian sport to pursue, as all my friends were more into that discipline and the Pony Club encouraged it. I would have preferred to just jump, but as I got older the show-jumping circuit seemed to be less friendly and more about prize money, whereas eventing still felt like a Pony Club excursion. Every week I would scour the ads at the back of *Horse & Hound* magazine to see what was for sale. It was fun to read the descriptions of the horses, and there were lots of them, but I had a particular type in mind. I waited patiently, and one day there was an ad for a nice-looking, 15.2-hand, Thoroughbred-cross gelding. He appeared to have everything I wanted; he had done some eventing with good results and was a good price. Mum and I jumped in the camper van and drove out to the countryside to see him.

Barnaby Rudge was the perfect size and age, and although he was finer than I'd had in mind, he looked the part. When we arrived, his owner was riding him around in a field; his head was down on the bit, and he had a big strong stride with lots of power. I asked the owner some questions about what experience he had, and she said he was unstoppable at cross-country and would jump anything. I liked the sound of that. She showed us some walk, trot and canter and then pointed him at a huge hedge between the fields. As soon as he saw that he was lined up for that hedge he sprang, zooming forward like he wanted to devour it. My jaw dropped open. He was stunning. The jump was about five feet high and he made it look like nothing. The rider turned him in a circle and jumped back into our field, smiled, jumped off and passed me the reins. It was all very impressive.

Now it was my turn to ride him and I was nervous. He looked like a lot of horse. But he went very well for me, listening to my aids, ears pointing forward, and I was pleased. After about ten minutes I turned him to a cross rail his owner had put up, but as soon as he saw it, he shot forward from underneath me and blasted over it. He did the same thing he had done over the hedge, taking off to get to the jump like his life depended on it. He went so fast I found myself getting left behind, scrambling to stay in the saddle. Like I was not even a part of the process and just holding on. I jumped the fence a couple more times and he took off each time. I asked the owner if he always did that, and she suggested that he loved his job and I just needed to get to know him better. I remember thinking that I didn't like the feeling, but maybe with training he might slow down.

I was fifteen by this point and thought I should know what I was doing. I didn't have a trainer with me or anyone to help me make the right choices. We had gone all that way to see him, and he was so handsome, and I didn't want to be rude...and I wanted a horse...and so...I asked my mum what she thought, and she said he was a beauty and she loved his name, so we made an offer and the owner said yes. The next weekend my dad and I drove to get him. He popped on the trailer, excited to be on a journey, and off we went.

All my friends were impressed when I got him back to Barwell; he was a serious-looking machine. But the first ride I took him on I got scared. He started bouncing around underneath me like he had lost his marbles. I tried to put it down to the fact that he needed to settle in, but I was frightened. He was so athletic and fast. The more I tried to stop him from leaping, the more threatening his behaviour became. He would literally throw himself sideways toward a fence or tree, and I'd have to turn him into his crazed direction, like controlling a skidding car. I thought about trying to return him because he didn't seem like the same horse I had tried the week before. But the next day he came up lame, limping to the gate when I went to catch him. He had a stone bruise on his hoof. This meant some time off for him and stall rest, and I couldn't return a lame horse. So I crossed my fingers and hoped for the best.

It was during this time that I decided to move out of Aunt Daphne's yard down to a small row of stables we called the lower barn. I was turning sixteen and I told myself I wanted more freedom, but I also wanted to hide. Things were getting a lot more serious and competitive in Aunt Daphne's yard. Some of my friends were doing well with their horses, and instead of being happy for them I was jealous. I couldn't deal with hearing about everyone's successes because they weren't mine. It didn't occur to me that when I had owned Stroller I was probably shown more attention; all I knew was that with Woofy I was lower-middle of the pack and I hated it. The conversation in my brain was getting too loud, and my solution was to leave.

This was a big change. It meant I was completely responsible for my horse without Aunt Daphne's watchful, mothering eye. My new yard had no one overseeing it, no one to answer to and no one to help. It was what I thought I wanted, but I started spending a lot of time on my own.

I had to arrange shavings, hay and grain, and my workload went up considerably, but I put my head down and looked after my horse. During the time Barnaby was lame, I poulticed his hoof and hand-grazed him every day. I got to know him. He was affectionate and sweet, and I started to grow in confidence. Surely he would look after me; he was my friend. When his hoof healed, I brought him back to work, schooling him in the sand ring and taking it slow. Things were going well. He was behaving and seemed much more relaxed, so one day I decided to take him out for a hack.

It was an ordinary grey British afternoon when we set out alone past the Racetrack Field and through the woods at the end of the bridle path. I tried to hide my nervousness from Barnaby by concentrating on the trees and navigating the mud. We were only walking, and when we reached the end of the woods I thought maybe that was far enough for now. So we turned for home. As with most horses, his pace picked up a little when he knew he was on the way back to the barn, but not enough to worry. His neck was long and low in front of me, ears pricked. As we got to the bridle path, his pace picked up another notch, so I gathered up the reins and moved him on into a trot. I thought if I could keep him busy and going forward it might stop him from getting excited. When we got to the hill, he put weight into the bridle, taking contact. I shortened my reins. Then he made a decision and broke into a canter. I pulled lightly to slow him down, but he didn't respond. I pulled harder, but nothing. A deep, slow panic seeped into my veins as he went faster and faster, like a train. I pulled again. Nothing. Time seemed to be slowing down, and I felt like I was shrinking, turning into a tiny mouse with huge eyes, sitting on his back, watching as the end of the track came rushing toward us. Everything went quiet except for this ferocious movement below me as he flattened out and really started to go. The end of the track meant the road, cars and the bridge over the highway.

I was frozen...it was coming.

I think it was the difference in footing, the clattering of metal shoes on tarmac, that broke the spell and snapped me into action. That's when I pulled frantically on the reins; I was fighting for my life now. I stood up in the stirrups and yanked on the bit with all my might. But he didn't slow at all. So I wrapped the reins around one of my fists and pulled hard with both hands, turning his head until it almost touched my knee. He couldn't see where he was going and he skidded, lurched, took a huge leap and finally stopped.

We stood, his rib cage heaving against my legs.

I could hear my heart thumping.

I was shaking all over.

I waited, summoning the courage to continue back to the yard.

I never told anyone about that day.

The trauma of that ride seeped deep into my bones. In a way, it was worse than if I had fallen off. My brain whirled, playing over and over all the things that could have happened but didn't. I sat imagining the what-ifs, like a playback loop of fear, wondering how much it would have hurt if he had skidded onto the dry road or crashed into the overpass bridge—and my mind was painting pictures that made it hard to sleep at night. I tried pretending it hadn't happened, putting the memory away, but it kept popping up like an uninvited guest. Instead of congratulating myself on pulling him up, I put it down to luck that we hadn't gotten hurt, that a car hadn't come around the corner at that moment. That I hadn't been thrown over the side of the overpass to my death below. As I had done before, I turned the knives on myself and started digging in.

From then on, riding Barnaby was a burden. Every time I put my foot in the stirrup, I had a certain amount of dread. The Crow was back, sitting on my head and causing mayhem, flapping its wings and squawking. I'd take a deep breath and act like I was tough, trying to seem confident, but as everyone always warned me, horses can smell fear. He could feel the tension in my seat and through my hands. I couldn't fool him. I was nervous and jumpy, and he knew it and became more nervous and jumpy because of it. We were on a slippery slope.

I didn't take him out hacking after that bolt, and I didn't tell any of my friends the reason why. My horsey life became more about training and less about fun. I wasn't going to give up, though. I was going to figure out this horse because he could jump anything. I thought that if I could gain control, I would have a winner. I kept riding four days a week, rain or shine, trying to figure it all out. I trained with a variety of instructors, but I could feel that bolt in him from then on, like his shadow in the sand, always with us.

A month or so later, I was having a riding lesson at my coach Lulu Med's house. Her family had converted their tennis court into a riding ring, and she kept her own two horses in the garage. I went there often. The riding ring was a little cramped and still had the chain-link fence, but the footing was good and it worked quite well. I was cantering around, working on transitions, when the same thing happened: suddenly Barnaby took over and started going faster and faster. Once again I went silent and still as he got a hold on the bit and took off. Lulu started yelling, "Turn his head to the wall! Pull him up!" but I couldn't. I couldn't move. I was frozen, except I was screaming inside. Finally she ran forward and stood in his way. That made him swerve and knocked him off his balance. He lost his momentum and slowed down.

Lulu looked at me. Up until then I think she had thought I was tough, but at that moment she saw how scared I was. She asked me what had just happened and I shrugged and mumbled something about Barnaby going too fast. I didn't want to let on the depth of the hopelessness I was feeling. She suggested I let her ride him for a few weeks, but I told her it was fine and that I'd be okay. Accepting help was, in my mind, an admission of defeat. I rode home gingerly, like I was sitting on a giant bomb with a lit match in my hand.

Day after day I worked with Barnaby, trying to trust him. I'd have the odd good ride, which would spur me on. But every time I lined him up for a jump, I'd feel like a passenger with a crazy pilot. We would always jump the fence, but too fast, and I had a big problem stopping him on the other side. After schooling him for a couple of months, I decided to take him to a local show to see if he would behave better off-property. Horses usually give you either more or less when you take them somewhere new. I entered him in a three-foot-six jumper class, hoping the fences would be big enough to slow him down. As I gathered my reins to take him at the first jump, he took off. He jumped the fence and galloped straight out of the ring, past the many spectators gathered at the entry gate. It was dangerous and I got yelled at as I tried to pull him up. I was mortified.

After that I stayed at Barwell as much as I could. I kept training, day after day, circle after circle. I avoided situations that would cause problems. But I was deflated, my passion dwindling. The whole point of having this horse was to compete, and the Pony Club would tempt me with fun events that I wanted to take part in. Eventually, my sense of adventure overcame my fear of calamity: I entered a cross-country schooling day and crossed my fingers.

A few weeks later, an excited bunch of us went in a horsebox to a cross-country facility near Sandown. We were all excited as we tacked up our horses and bandaged their legs. We mounted and rode out into a huge misty field, where the instructor started helping us warm up. I was feeling hopeful, and all was going well, but as soon as we started jumping, Barnaby got overexcited. He started prancing around before every jump, leaping and bounding, distracting everyone else as I held on for dear life. The instructor kept saying, "Stop holding him back—just go!" but I couldn't. I simply didn't trust him. It was like standing on the edge of a diving board and not having the guts to jump. I was teetering, my heart hammering in my chest. Barnaby began rooting, diving down on the bit, shaking his head, ears pinned back, and I froze.

Suddenly the instructor shouted, "STOP. STOP RIGHT NOW!" Everyone pulled up and looked around. She walked over to me and took hold of Barnaby's reins, then shook my leg and said, "Breathe." I started breathing in huge gulps, then crying and finally bawling. I was miserable and scared.

Luckily the instructor was kind and took pity on me. She told me to get off and sit this one out. I sat miserably and watched everyone else galloping around, having fun. Later one of my friends told me I had gone quite blue. After the lesson the instructor asked if I'd like to stay on at her farm for a few days so we could try to figure out why Barnaby was being so difficult. I knew I was holding him back and he needed to go forward, but I also thought that if I let the reins soften, he might take off.

I kept saying to her, "Maybe it's me."

My friends put their horses in the horsebox and went back to Barwell, and I stayed on. After another bad lesson the next morning, the instructor had an interesting idea. To this day I am still not sure how she got me to agree to it, but it shows how much I wanted to succeed. Her idea was to take Barnaby to Epsom Downs Racecourse that afternoon and gallop him until he could go no farther. Epsom Downs is a famous racetrack in England and has miles and miles of open track. It's stunning, with long sweeping hills as far as the eye can see. We drove Barnaby to the Downs in her trailer and got ready. I was trying to be upbeat, pretending this was going to be fun, but I was drowning in fear. The instructor handed me my crash helmet and a spine protection vest, then said, "Get on and push him into a gallop so that it's your choice. Then let him go and we'll see how long he runs for."

Gulp. I got on and he took off. I don't think I had it in me to push him forward, and I didn't need to. He just went, flat out in a gallop, from zero to sixty, his ears pinned back. My eyes started watering from the rush of cold air. I wrapped some mane around my right glove and held on. The wind filled my ears with a sound like an airplane taking off, and as he pounded forward I could feel myself shrinking, disappearing into my eye sockets. It went on and on, this thunderous motion below me, the Downs slipping past under his beating hooves. But after a while a funny thing happened. I got used to the speed. There was nothing around us, no obstacles to run into or fall over. The world stretched out in front of us, like a blank piece of paper, and slowed down; it was like flying in a cloudless sky. My fear began to ease as my legs started to burn from balancing above his back like a racing jockey. The rhythm started to drop off, and he eventually drifted back into an awkward trot, then walk. I was talking to him now, "Good boy, that was good, that's right, let's walk now…"

I can't remember how far we went, but it was a long way. Then I cautiously turned him for home. As soon as we rounded the corner he took off again, and we galloped all the way back. He was dripping and steaming by the end of it and so was I. When I got off, I could barely stand; my legs were like jelly. We cooled him off, put him back on the trailer and took him back to the farm, where I crawled into bed.

The next morning Barnaby had a different look in his eyes. My instructor wondered if he had been frustrated. We took him back to the Downs and repeated the exercise, but this time he didn't gallop as far, and on the way home he started trotting. He was tired. On the third day we did our cross-country schooling lesson over the same course that we had sat out on three days before, and he was good.

Success.

When we flew
I handed you
my head
my trust

You kept running
till your heart beat slower
and your head dropped lower

For a moment
But moments
are moments
after all

When I took him back to Barwell, I had two weeks of normal horse. I was ecstatic! But then that look in his eye started to come back. I tried to hire someone to gallop him for me. Although I had proven to myself that I had it in me, I hated doing it—but nobody else wanted to do it either. I got into a routine where the day before an event I'd take him to a big field, hold my breath and let him run. I'd put him in a bridle with a more severe bit called a Pelham,* which had an extra rein on the bottom, a levered bit and a curb chain. We didn't like using bits like this in the Pony Club, and I was always afraid that he might rear, but I didn't have Epsom Downs and I needed to stop at the end of the field. If he wouldn't pull up, I'd pull that other rein and he would leap, plunge and stop dead. It wasn't fun at all. I now had control, but it was mayhem onboard. My friends would watch me and say, "He's crazy."

I had found the key for Barnaby and I started taking him to events and doing well. But I hadn't found the key to turn off my nerves. They now became the shadow that followed us along, but the shadow had talons, and they were digging into the back of my neck.

This was a time of transition. As I sank into my mid-teens, ponies were sold and replaced by gangly, spotty boys. I was a hopeless romantic and would dream for hours about boys I'd never even met. If I watched a romantic movie, I could spend weeks thinking about it, completely immersed in the tragedy. One day I fell totally in love with a boy who walked past me on my way to school. I thought he was the one true love of my life, and I walked every day that same way, at the same time, trying to catch another glimpse of him. I drew his name, which I made up, on my pencil case, and my heart would hurt just thinking about him. I was brimming with emotion and I had no idea where to put it.

When I was fifteen and a half, my father left home for a much younger woman. He told me in passing when I was cleaning the vw camper in our courtyard. I watched him walk out of the Kerry Stables gates and a canyon opened up in my chest and swallowed my heart. My dad was my hero; he was the leader of our family and the one I relied on. There had been a lot of fighting between my parents, and my mother's drinking was bad, but I never thought he would actually leave. After that I only saw him for lunch once a week, and everything in my world started to fall apart. As if we were in a Hollywood movie, the Kerry Stables roof leaked even more, and the paint cracked and peeled from the walls. The windows got dirty and the grass was never mowed. We no longer gathered at the kitchen table, which was always covered with newspapers, milk bottles, the ironing—just stuff. My mother would be drunk by mid-afternoon every day, and our dogs were on edge and barked at night. Something big was over and I couldn't see light anymore.

It was my final year at Putney High School, and I made a big show of not caring about anything. In England, at age sixteen you take O-levels, standardized exams that indicate whether you are ready to go on to higher-level education (the A-levels) or to college. I finished the year with only one O-level, which was unheard of, and from then on I held the record for the lowest number of exams passed by any student in the history of my school. This meant I had no option of going into higher education, so I started to look for a job. I ended up getting hired at a fish-and-chips take-away. It was miserable; I started to smell like a deep-fat fryer and gained weight. Each shift felt like an eternity and my boss always found a reason to shout at me. I couldn't blame her, though; I was terrible at working the register. It was impossible for me, like school. I couldn't seem to focus and would screw up over and over again.

My dad did not like this turn of events and looked around for a solution. I have no idea how he managed it, but he got me accepted at art school. For the next couple of years I took Graphic Techniques at Richmond Art College, but I struggled to keep up at that too. I was no good at anything and it didn't matter anymore. I got comfortable in my gloom, grabbed a shovel and dug myself a big hole to lie in.

I still rode Barnaby and went to the odd competition, but my dreams of being a professional rider were dissolving. I had friends who were, in my mind, far more fearless. I would compare myself with them and beat myself up. After my father left home, money also became much more of an issue. I knew the days of having my own horse were numbered.

Then one Saturday I was watching the telly and Badminton horse trials came on. Badminton is a big deal in eventing—sort of the same as Wimbledon is to tennis. It brings out all the top riders from around the world and pits them against each other over a particularly hair-raising cross-country course. If you get to Badminton, you've made it. The three-day event is set on stunning grounds in the heart of Gloucestershire, home to the Duke and Duchess of Beaufort. You can usually spot a few Royals with binoculars, leaning on their shooting sticks or standing beside Land Rovers, taking in the event. In fact, I had stood about thirty feet from the Queen herself with my Barwell friends whilst watching our hero Lucinda Green on Regal Realm win the year before.

As I sat in my big room and watched the cross-country segment of the competition, I started to get that feeling in my stomach, a mixture of adrenaline, fear and excitement, and I thought to myself, "I need to compete." If I could start winning, maybe I could turn everything around. If I was successful, maybe everything would be better again. I had to do something. I had to make some sense of my horse journey. So I came up with a plan, rolled up my sleeves and entered Barnaby in a massive competition, a qualifier for the Great Britain cross-country championships. I had acquired enough points to enter, and I thought, "Sod it," and started training again. I got Barnaby fit, jumping him twice a week and taking him for regular gallops. I was determined and moving forward. The plan was in action.

As the event date got closer, I was ready. I wanted to have the same feeling I'd had entering the ring on Stroller. I needed something to go right. I didn't tell my coach or any of my friends that I was going to go to this event. I knew everyone would call me crazy, but I needed to do it for my mum and dad, and also for Barnaby. We all needed it.

Finally, after four weeks of ramping up my training, it was show day and I was prepared. I'd breezed Barnaby the day before, taking him for that gallop to clear his mind. I'd bathed him and given him breakfast. We were ready and it was going to be perfect.

My dad hitched up the trailer and we loaded Barnaby on, wheeled on my tack trunk and drove away down the lane. Two hours later we arrived at the showgrounds—and it was the wrong day. A day early. My heart started to fall. I have done this many times in my life. I think it's because I get so worried about wasting other people's time that I start to mix myself up and consequently waste *more* of other people's time. My dad was not pleased to find only a few people walking the course and no one on horseback. But being nothing if not opportunistic, he decided that we would make the most of things and stay overnight with a friend of his who had a farm nearby. What could I say? I went along with it, knowing I didn't have anything my horse needed, like enough hay or grain. We put Barnaby in a grassy field with some water. He looked okay, so I tried not to worry and went to bed.

The next morning we went back to the showgrounds and I walked the course. It was huge and I was shaking with fear by the end. I knew Barnaby could do it; it wouldn't be fun, but he would jump anything I pointed him at. I just had to hold on. I got into my gear and headed down to the ring beside the start gate and did my usual warm-up, which included walk, trot, canter and a few jumps. Barnaby was feeling good, maybe a little tired, but that was a relief because he wasn't being "crazy."

Everyone in the warm-up ring looked serious. It was a British Horse Society event and I wondered if I might be out of my league. I also didn't understand some of the rules. But the hunger was coming back to me; that "I'm going to show them" feeling was pumping through my veins, and I was excited to get going. My ride time was 2:10 p.m. and I was ready, but as I got to the start gate the announcer said there was a delay, so I had to wait. I sat in the warm-up ring until 2:30 p.m. and then took Barnaby back to the trailer. I didn't know that during that time I was meant to go down and check the jump order. After another forty-five minutes the announcer called my number. I jumped back on board and trotted down to the start gate, where a paunchy man in a flat cap and a clip-board said, "Ready, NOW GO!" and clicked his stopwatch.

"WHAT?!" I said. "But I haven't warmed up!"

He kept saying, "You have to go NOW—your time is running!"

I went.

I pushed Barnaby forward through the start gate, but he was not ready. He was lethargic, like he had no idea we were competing. Nothing like the dragon I usually rode.

The first fence was called a tiger trap. It's built like a triangular wooden cage. This one had a gap of about three feet at the top and was about three-feet-three-inches high. Horses like these jumps, and they are considered inviting. We were going toward it and he didn't feel awake, so I gave him a kick. I had never, ever had to kick him, and he did the strangest thing: he started to jump. We were still about two strides away from the fence—way too far away to clear it. I grabbed hold of his mane and thought, "SHIIIIIT." I watched in slow motion as his front legs went right into the middle of the jump, and I was then catapulted forward as his hind legs came flying over his head. I landed on the other side of the fence on my back, looking up at the clouds. Time was moving very slowly, and I remember thinking, "I'm such an idiot." Then I looked over and there was Barnaby, also on his back looking up at the clouds, pawing the air, long strips of flesh hanging from his legs. He looked terrified. My poor horse.

I couldn't move, and then this strange sound started coming from my mouth; I wailed. Barnaby looked so frightened, and I was so annoyed with myself and frustrated. Everything came screaming out of me. Why couldn't it have been amazing? Why couldn't we have been successful? Why?

I think when you make something too important in your mind, you can often curse it. I rode the success in my head so many times that it was bound to fail. I needed it too much to succeed.

I was driven off the field in an ambulance. The paramedics wanted to check my spine. We had what is called a full rotational fall—the same fall as movie star Christopher Reeve (*Superman*) had while eventing, which, tragically, paralyzed him.

I was in bad shape. They said I had five vertebrae out of place. But nothing was broken—except me. Something deep down in me had relented, and I said goodbye to the girl who had dreams. I told her that life was crap and not to bother trying.

Barnaby was okay. His legs healed as my back mended, but I didn't feel like riding him after that. I'd go up to the farm and groom him. I couldn't put myself through any more fear…I didn't want to get back on. After a while I decided it was time to sell him. I knew it wasn't his fault. The whole journey up to the first fence that day was a travesty of bad planning on my part. I was so angry with myself. But I was tired of trying.

I wrote an ad and sent it in to *Horse & Hound*, but when people would call, I couldn't lie. I'd tell them he was difficult, and that would put them off even coming to try him out. So he sat in the field, and I started to pretend he wasn't there. Weeks would go by and I wouldn't visit him. But it wasn't easy, being neglectful. I'd think about him all the time and feel awful and full of shame.

My mum clued in, though. She barely seemed to notice what I was doing most of the time, but when I stopped going to the barn she got angry. She always stood up for the animals and couldn't stand the thought of me not looking after my horse. One day she decided enough was enough. She hitched up the horse trailer and we took Barnaby to a sales barn. To me, sales barns were like shady used-car dealers. I had never even been to one before that point because they didn't have a good reputation. Horses were money to them, that was all. Mum hated them too, but at least Barnaby would be looked after.

I hadn't ridden him for about six weeks when we took him. It was a long trailer ride, and I remember it was also extremely hot. When we got there and took him out of the trailer, he looked tired. The people at the sales barn tacked him up and rode him around and he behaved perfectly. He did a course of jumps like he was a schoolmaster and stood quietly as the girl dismounted. I shrugged; it was a good day. I told them all about him, that he bolted sometimes and that he was tricky. They said he went well and was not a problem. I told them that he could be dangerous for a novice rider. They shrugged. They looked at me as though I was stupid and obviously didn't know what I was talking about. They gave me half of what I thought he was worth, and we walked away. I didn't say anything on the way home.

About three weeks later the sales barn people phoned and asked for me. They said Barnaby had bolted up the road and put a girl rider in hospital. They said he was dangerous and I should take him back. My mum grabbed the phone and yelled at them, "We told you everything and you didn't listen. He's your problem now!" and she hung up. I looked at her. I would have taken him back.

"Problem horse," I thought and hung my head. I remembered him lying on his back after our big fall and wondered for the first time if he had just been scared. Whether all the bolting and leaping around was not him being crazy, but him being terrified, like me.

I felt bad about the whole thing. Maybe he would have been okay with a bolder rider. Maybe I should have tried harder. Maybe he was a winner and I wrecked him.

It didn't occur to me that Barnaby was an off-the-track Thoroughbred, that he had been taught to run. That running was his job. That I had been lied to when I bought him. That maybe being trusting isn't a fault. That maybe the woman who sold him to me, who lied to me, was at fault. It didn't occur to me because I was wading through a porridge of self-doubt, so of course I could do nothing but blame myself.

I stopped riding at that point. I don't think I said goodbye to anyone at Barwell. I just didn't go back. Most of my Pony Club friends had also moved on.

We all went our separate ways, and I stopped thinking about horses.

But the strange thing is, horses kept walking back into my life.

CHAPTER 5

Sonnet, 1999–2009

Tamara, thirty-two years old

He stands alone
in his costume of spots and tinges of gold
He takes me anywhere with certainty
He is so strong
that I hand it all over...
Here take my day and throw it away
Let's pound through the fields and march along trails
that lead to clear
simple
evenings

As my horse dreams faded away, a passion for writing songs took hold. I'd always found music was a place in which I could float. It would sweep me away; my brain and I would be swamped in the different lands and waves of noise. I'd lie for hours, melting into recordings with all their intricate production ideas. I'd go deep into the sonics, listening over and over to the same song until I knew every millisecond of its form. Music had the ability to completely overcome my busy mind and cover me like a warm, fuzzy blanket, making me feel okay.

Sonnet in front of the house we rented.

I was eighteen, still living at home, and my relationship with my mother was simply crappy. She had given herself a massive make-over and was dating and trying to make out that she was loving it, but it all looked sad and desperate from where I stood. One day, when she tipped over in the kitchen and was too drunk to get up, I came to the conclusion that I actually hated her. Because of the divorce, my parents had cut the Kerry Stables property in half and sold off the beautiful part. That part, where we had been born and grew up, was now behind a high wall. My mum, Ben and I lived in the extension side of the house, in what used to be our playroom. I had a tiny bedroom, not much bigger than my bed, and a closet. I hated it and missed our old home. But the real end of my ability to cope with things came when my brother Ben went to university. We had always relied on each other, and his departure was a mas-sive blow for me. He was the buffer between me and my mum, so when he left it was like the floor of my world had been removed.

My relationship with my father was also changing because his new girlfriend was encouraging him to be firm with me and treat me like an adult. It felt like he had deserted me just when I needed him the most. He was totally in love with this new woman, so I saw him less and less, and when I did see him, she would be there. Needless to say, I couldn't stand her. She was a self-professed intel-lectual and, right away, that made me think she wasn't. On one occasion I remember going to my dad's apartment to play four new songs I had written, and she got out a notepad so she could give me her feedback in notation at the end of my performance. I, er…yeah.

It was then I got a new companion along with my depression, and her name was anger. She sat in my throat and at the back of my eyes and looked out at my future and painted it many shades of grey.

But this was also a time of rebirth for me. I started to write music with two amazing songwriters, Sean Hughes and Nigel Brown, both of whom taught me tons. I loved them dearly. Nigel, who became my boyfriend for a while, was a sweet guy and a talented guitarist. We started a band and I was introduced to the world that is a recording studio. I learned about reverb and delays, and it was like someone had opened two big doors at the sides of my brain; I had to go and explore. I loved using my ears, and I noticed that when I was working with music, people around me started to listen and take me seriously. What amazed me about this was that I wasn't even trying. Ideas would fly from me before I'd even thought of them. Music was a language I spoke; it was easy.

When I left art college, my dad found me a job at an advertising agency right in the heart of London. It was chic, swanky and exciting. I met a bunch of new friends and we started having amazing dinner parties and enjoying London. A large part of the English condition, in addition to dogs and horses, is drinking, and by this point I was no stranger to the local pub. But this group of friends took drinking to a new level. We would drink right through fun and mayhem until we blacked out on the living room floor. We were all so energized and excited around each other that we couldn't seem to control ourselves. It was a crazy few years of feeling on fire.

By 1990 Margaret Thatcher had been leading the country into or out of recession for what seemed like forever. Britain felt downtrodden and gloomy. At some point I lost my job, which led to many others: photography assistant, waitress, sandwich maker, moving company schlep, pub server. I was useless at all these jobs and, as usual, couldn't concentrate. If they started well, I'd get more and more nervous, waiting for a big blunder to materialize, and it never let me down. Whether it was spilling tea on the photographer's negatives or getting orders wrong at the pub, I'd just cock up. Eventually I gave up trying and went on the dole, which was like living permanently in a punk rock song.

After a while my mad new group of friends started to go their different ways, and I decided it was time to leave home. I talked to my boyfriend, Nigel, about moving in together, and we looked at a flat right next to Hammersmith roundabout, which is said to be one of the busiest roundabouts in Europe. The flat was tiny and noisy, and it smelled of mould. The windows were covered in dark-grey grime from the endless traffic outside, and it had a shared bathroom where you had to put fifty pence in to heat the water. I wasn't ready for that. Nigel was a sweet guy and a kind boyfriend, and I'm sure we could have built a lovely future together, but when I looked at that apartment, I knew I couldn't do it. The next day, walking up Putney Hill after visiting a thrift store, I thought, "That's it, I'm done."

When I was a small girl, we'd had lodgers and relatives stay at the Kerry Stables. One of them had been Chris de Burgh, who was now a famous pop star. My dad had helped him get started with his amazing career, so I reached out to him and asked how I could get my music career going. He suggested I move out of London. When I told him I was thinking of Canada, he told me that he loved playing music in Toronto and that there was a pumping music scene there. Two weeks later, on May 3, 1991, I stuffed my backpack full of clothes, grabbed my guitar and jumped on a plane across the pond.

This was an easy move. I had dual citizenship because my dad was a Canadian. My eldest brother lived in Toronto at the time, so I could stay with him. I'd visited a few times and made some friends, so I thought I'd live in Canada for the summer and see what it was like.

The day I arrived, I picked up a local entertainment paper called *NOW* and saw a Singer Wanted ad; the very next day I joined a band called Garden Traffic. The other members were lovely young guys in their last year of high school, and they became my new family. They were all gifted musicians and already had some amazing song ideas. We started doing well, and before I knew it we were playing some of the biggest stages in Toronto, making music videos and an album. My music career set sail.

A year later, after they all left for university, I met a new bass player and drummer and we started a band called Mrs. Torrance. Before the first year was out, we were signed to a major label. Again, I loved the guys in my band and they became my brothers. Together we released albums and toured from coast to coast, playing festivals and sharing the bill with bands like Oasis, the Beautiful South and Jewel. It was an incredible time in music. The Toronto scene was jumping, and Queen Street was alive; I made tons of friends and had a ridiculous amount of fun. I was good at something at last, and I belonged. I said goodbye to Tammy and used my real name, Tamara. I was armed with a distortion pedal, a Gibson SG, my anger and one hell of a rhythm section. I was winning at last.

About six months after I arrived in Canada, Barnaby came back to haunt me. He appeared in my dreams one night and then visited every month or so. I hadn't thought about him for years; I was heavily into my new life. But there he was, walking toward me with his head low and huge overgrown feet curling over like in an advertisement for abused horses. I'd shrink away in my dream and wake up miserable. I didn't know what I could do. He was gone and I had no idea how to find him.

After a year of dealing with this dream, I spoke to a friend who was a therapist. He suggested that the next time the dream came to me, I needed to say sorry; maybe I had to write a song or paint a picture, but I had to forgive myself for that period of my life. I smiled and thought, "That sounds kind of lame." I thought I should be tough and just handle it, but the dream kept hounding me. One day, as I was out running, I saw Barnaby again, crawling along in my mind, hobbling in pain toward me. I kept running, tears rolling down my cheeks, until I saw a park bench. Then I sat down and sobbed. I remembered all the times he had taken off and jumped around, the times I'd groomed him and stroked his nose. The bad communication as he panicked beneath me, all the fear that I'd swallowed and tried not to show. I said sorry to him in my head and told myself I'd done my best with what I had to offer at that time, and he slowly faded away.

By the late 1990s my career as a musician was changing. The internet had come into play: streaming services took over from selling albums in music stores. Musicians started to lose record deals and had to rely on touring and self-management. My band was dropped from its deal with BMG and I lost my support network. I released some solo records and had some tours, but it was the end of an era. I was heading into my thirties, unsure of where my career in music was going. As a band we'd had hundreds of thousands of dollars pass through our books, and I'd played in front of thousands of people, yet I was still having trouble paying my rent. I had been in a relationship with an incredible, well-known Canadian musician, but it had ended and my heart was broken in two. And years of touring and staying out late had taken their toll; I was weak and flimsy. But just when I most needed it, a series of events brought horses back into my life.

One evening at a party at my brother Robbie's house, I met a strapping young man who told me his sister had some horses. I started telling him all about my horse life in England and how much I loved riding. I was probably going on a bit, but he listened intently and then invited me out to his sister's farm the next week. I was elated. The thought of getting back on a horse was so exciting. Until that moment I hadn't realized that the area north of Toronto was horse heaven: huge forests, farmland and loads of horse-boarding facilities.

The next weekend I jumped on the back of the strapping young man's motorcycle and went to meet his sister, Jabette, on her farm in Stouffville. Jabette had two horses, Jamie and Bianca. They were her pets and lived out behind her lovely century-old farmhouse in a paddock with a run-in shed. I hadn't been up close to a horse in eight years and I could hardly wait to meet them. When we walked out to the field, the horses trotted over, their ears forward. I held my breath for a moment as their beautiful big heads nuzzled me, looking for treats. They smelled like sweet grass and fresh soil. I gave them carrots and touched their soft noses with the palm of my hand and stroked their long, smooth necks. They were beautiful horses, and I stood with them for quite a while, taking it all in as the sun set over the cornfields on the horizon behind the farm.

I exhaled.

The next morning Jabette invited me to go for a hack and I said yes before she finished the sentence. I couldn't wait to ride again. I didn't for a second feel any fear or trepidation, and sitting in the saddle was like going home. My body and mind relaxed as though they had forgotten fear, and I wondered if I had left the Crow behind me in England.

That first ride was the start of a wonderful friendship. I would regularly take the bus north up Yonge Street and spend the weekend with Jabette and her partner, Brett. We would set off and ride into the woods and along massive fields with abandoned farmhouses and empty bank barns. Developers were buying up land around Toronto and leaving it sitting empty. It was a shame, but at the same time it was perfect for exploring on horseback. I loved going to the farm. Brett and Jabette would invite a pile of friends up to swim in the pond near their farm and then cook incredibly delicious meals. We would sit at the table for hours and eat homemade pasta and lots of yummy buttery French dishes. It became my favourite thing to do on any given weekend, and I started to feel stronger.

After going up and hacking for a year or so, it dawned on me that I could become a part-time riding instructor. I thought maybe I had something to offer that would earn me more than the minimum-wage jobs I usually ended up getting in Toronto. Stouffville had a local feed store with everything farm related, so I popped in and saw an ad for an instructor wanted at a nearby equestrian facility. I called the number and a woman with a Cockney accent answered. Her name was Joyce and I liked her immediately. When I went for the interview and told Joyce I'd grown up in the Pony Club, she smiled, shook my hand and gave me the job on the spot.

Joyce was an amazing character. She was tiny, in her mid-seventies, but looked about eleven years old from behind. She had brassy blond hair, wore a bright-pink puffy jacket and walked like her upper body had left her legs two feet behind. She ran a board-ing facility and riding school on her own; she had twelve boarders and several older school horses that she taught kids on. The barn was old and falling apart, but she kept it tidy, and it had a friendly atmosphere. There were about twenty stalls, tucked all around the place, and an indoor riding arena. The farm was about fifty acres, some of which was paddocks, with an indoor arena, an outdoor sand ring and a large pond. There was also a small bungalow on site, where Joyce lived.

Joyce was a hard worker. She had no tractor or machinery to help her with chores; she did everything with a wheelbarrow and elbow grease. I learned very quickly to do things her way and keep my head down. She was like a small tornado, always mov-ing through the barn and shouting at everyone and everything if things weren't done exactly right. At the same time she had a twin-kle in her eye and was very funny and full of life. The animals and I loved her.

Going to Joyce's became the highlight of my week. I'd teach all day Saturday and Sunday, breathing in the clean air, grooming and working with the horses and kids. I'd arrive back home in Toronto on Sunday night with rosy cheeks and a feeling of contentment that I only ever found after a day with my four-legged friends.

All of Joyce's school horses were well-behaved, but one afternoon after I had finished teaching a lesson, Joyce asked me if I wouldn't mind getting on a horse called Sonnet because he was scaring the kids with the odd buck. "Oh god," I thought. I didn't want to get thrown off either, but I agreed because I didn't want to lose my job. She disappeared into the barn and a few minutes later came out leading an Appaloosa. This is a breed of spotted horses from North America whose ancestors can be seen in ancient cave paintings in Greece and China. Appaloosas are derived from a Spanish horse crossed with a mustang, and you usually see them in old cowboy movies being ridden by Native American warriors. Nowadays they are one of the most popular horse breeds in the United States. They are considered tough, strong and very hardy.

Until that moment I hadn't thought much of "Appies," as they are affectionately known. We had a few in England, but in our snobby British way we thought they were for cowboys. Sonnet was a whitish-golden colour, with a black mane that stood straight up in the air. He had pink skin around his strangely human eyes, and a pink spotted nose. He looked stunning, like a serious work of art, and was obviously very proud. I popped on him and instantly thought, "Wow!" He felt so good—smooth and easy to ride. He gave me no trouble at all and was well-schooled. Joyce suggested that I start riding him regularly so he might behave himself better for her students, and I accepted without hesitation.

The very next day I asked if I could take him for a quick hack, and Joyce readily agreed. As I rode away from the barn, I knew we were going to have fun because he was completely relaxed, with his ears pointed forward, as if he were smiling. Some horses don't like leaving the barn on their own—they get nervous away from their friends—but not Sonnet. We were marching together on a journey like fearless explorers. The only problem was that I was having so much fun I forgot to keep track of where we were, and we got hopelessly lost. We were going across train tracks, down steep hills and along busy roads. Eventually we ended up in a cornfield where the corn was way up over both our heads, but he just soldiered on. I could walk, trot and canter, and he went wherever I wanted; he was happy to do anything I asked, and I fell in love. Every horse is different and I'd never had a horse this confident before. He was so uncomplicated and strong; he glided across the ground like a sofa on wheels and only looked forward.

When I got back to the barn, Joyce screamed at me because I'd been gone for almost two hours. When I told her all about how lost I had been and how amazing Sonnet was, she got a huge grin on her tiny face. Sonnet and I had had a great adventure, and I slept that night like I'd won a war. The horse bug had bitten me again.

During the week, when I wasn't teaching riding, I got a job working for a landscaping company in Toronto. It was a small group of misfits, artists and students cleaning up and planting high-end gardens in the wealthy Rosedale area. It was hard work but we had a blast and were constantly being stupid and laughing. I loved it.

The head of the crew was a ridiculously handsome young man who looked like a young Paul Newman. He had blond buzzed hair, a chiselled jawline and a physique that you usually only saw on a soap opera. He was very shy, and his face looked like it hadn't smiled enough. After a while I noticed that he never laughed out loud. He often sat apart from the group, eating his lunch quietly and looking away into the distance. I decided it would be my mission to get him to join in with us other workers, so I started chatting with him, asking him questions as we weeded gardens. He turned out to be a very clever guy who knew everything about horticulture. He spent hours every night after work planting seeds on his own in a greenhouse. He was eccentric and passionate about gardening, and I liked him. As the months wore on we started talking more and more in the van on the way back from the worksites. We shared similar childhood experiences, but some of his memories knocked my stories out of the park, and I began to understand why he was such a loner. I don't know if I was the first girl who actually got close to him, but one day he bought me a sandwich at the food truck and gave me *that* look.

I was thirty-two by this time, and he was six years younger than me. I hadn't thought about him romantically because he seemed like he was from a different generation. I had had this life as a musician and been all over the place, and he was a sweet Canadian boy, growing flowers in a greenhouse. Over the summer we had become friends; I cared about him. Then one day he asked me out for a drink and I thought, "Well, I'll go, just for fun." Over our second glass of wine he told me flat out that I was going to spend the rest of my life with him. I laughed and said, "Really?" And then, as the evening wore on, I found myself liking the idea. He walked me home and held my hand, and at my front door I looked straight into his bright blue eyes and dove in. I liked how sure he was. I wasn't sure of anything. Maybe that's what would make me happy. A man who was sure. He was also so beautiful that I had to try.

As well as landscaping and teaching riding, I was still playing the odd show with my own band and doing occasional tours with an incredible group called King Cobb Steelie. But my music career was ebbing away. By this time I was living in my grandmother's house up in North Toronto, keeping an eye on her. My brother had moved back to England, so Gran was my only family left in Toronto. She was a tough old bird, in her nineties, with a sharp mind and whip-like humour, but she was getting on. We would go out to see a movie like *Terminator*, and then she would take me for a fancy dinner and drink me under the table. I loved visiting her, but living with her was a different story. I thought it would be okay if I lived in her basement and helped her with cooking and cleaning, but she hated me being in her space and it was a bit of a nightmare. Then one day she had a big fall, and the doctor decided it would be safer for her to move into a care home. I stayed on at her house for the next year or so, until my father decided to sell it. So there I was, thirty-two with nowhere to live, a new boyfriend who loved plants, my love for horses returning and my music career fizzling out. I was sitting at a crossroads with nothing holding me back, so it didn't take long for me to choose a new direction.

Driving up to Joyce's each week, I'd see empty farmhouses with rental signs in front of them, and I started to fantasize about a whole new life. I wanted to get up in the mornings and look out the window and see green fields and big old trees. I'd been living in cities my whole life and I was ready for change. Like clockwork, a hand-drawn For Rent sign popped up on the sheep farm opposite Joyce's barn.

The sign was sitting at the end of a long driveway that led to a tall, white century house sitting by a field with a barn beside it. The place had obviously been leased for many years and was somewhat rundown, but it was a classic Ontario farm. I phoned the number and met with the owner the next day. The house was dauntingly huge after my small Toronto apartments, with four bedrooms, high ceilings, a traditional staircase with banisters and a big wood stove. There were many outbuildings, and sheep grazed happily in the fields. It came with the barn and two paddocks, which added up to about two acres of land. Part of me wondered if it was too much, but I signed the rental agreement and pretended I knew what I was doing. A few weeks later, with trepidation and excitement, I moved in with my boyfriend and a couple of other friends. It was a big new life and we had lots to do as we settled in and became country folk; we had fires in the wood stove, planted vegetables and ate apple pies. We got ourselves a big dog and went for long walks under the stars. I gained weight and looked like a farm girl again, and my guitar collected dust under the kitchen table.

Almost every day I would walk to Joyce's to work, help out and ride Sonnet. Her barn was a social hub, with lots of hustle and bustle, and she ran a good riding school business. She fussed over the kids, and I could tell she was transported back in time to when she was a Pony Clubber, just as I was. We had that in common, our English riding roots.

I had been out of horses for long enough that I needed to both relearn things and also understand the Canadian way of doing things. For instance, in England we tied the horses to a piece of baling twine attached to a ring on a post; in Canada they use cross ties. Canadians call stables "stalls" and head collars "halters," and on the bridle, they call the throat lash a "throat latch." There were differences in the way the children learned to ride as well, because they rode hunter classes, which we didn't have in England. I also noticed a lack of tweed and polished boots. There were a lot of puffy jackets and jeans about, and when winter hit, I started riding in ski pants, which I never would have dreamed of doing back home.

Joyce's horses required a lot of care, partly because they spent the night in the barn instead of living outdoors 24/7, which meant mucking stalls and turning the horses in and out, putting on rugs, and … well, there were lots of jobs to do. When each horse must have a specific amount of grain and different supplements, feeding twenty horses can take a long time. Feeding the wrong food at the wrong time can lead to colic, which can be deadly. And because Joyce boarded other people's horses, I had to deal with the owners. I think it's fair to say that some people get along better with their cats than with other people; the same applies to horse owners, so looking after their horses came with a lot of responsibility. For staff, like me, it was similar to babysitting. Each owner's horse was incredibly special to them, and they wanted to have individualized special care. The owners weren't a very laid-back bunch, and they doted on their horses, spending large amounts of money on massages and regular chiropractor treatments. I'm sure they didn't fork out money to get that kind of attention for themselves. They put all this work and money into their animals, but a lot of them seldom rode, which seemed counterintuitive to me. As time went on, I realized that these were horse enthusiasts, not riders. They loved their horses and wanted to take care of them, but improving their riding skills was not part of their journey.

Sonnet was a well-schooled horse, and I could tell he had been a jumper at some point. When you find a nice horse in a riding school, there is usually a reason. With Sonnet it was his conformation. Conformation is the way a horse's body is set up. Like people, horses are all different: some have a short back and a long neck, while others have the opposite; some look like they are sloping uphill, some down; some have floppy ears, and so on. This makes for different strengths and weaknesses. For instance, a horse with a long back can often jump more easily. If they have faults with their legs, you can run into soundness issues. Sonnet had pigeon toes. If you stood straight in front of him, you could see his feet turning in, which put a lot of strain on his tendons. With careful trimming and a good blacksmith you can help a horse like this, but Sonnet had had years in a riding school with not much attention paid to his feet. Because he wasn't my horse, I didn't think too much about it. I used to ride him out in the deep snow, bounding along like we were floating, but it wasn't long before he went lame and had to have some time off. I felt ashamed that I hadn't been more cautious, but I had no idea deep snow could be so tough on a horse.

By then I was the only one who was riding him because he was still misbehaving too much to be in the lesson program. He was perfect with me, but as soon as a kid got on he would shake his head and start rounding his back like he was going to buck them off. It was very naughty but I loved him for it. Joyce could see I adored him, so she asked if I wanted to lease him from her in exchange for teaching lessons and I agreed. He was such a character. I'd bandage his legs each night with cooling clay poultice, and he would nibble my jacket and lick my head.

It was like he had chosen me to be his mum.

I'd been living at my new farm for about nine months before I noticed Joyce was getting into financial trouble. She'd make the odd comment about the increasing cost of hay, but she never let on about her situation or complained. Then one morning she announced that she had to close shop, move and give all her school horses back to the local horse supplier. She said it to me like she was asking me to go fetch her a bale of hay, but our eyes locked for the briefest of moments and I could see how heartbroken she was. I knew Joyce would be okay—she was a survivor—but I still couldn't believe it. She would have to have a complete change of lifestyle and move into town. All the boarders would have to find new barns and go their separate ways. Everything was going to change.

I admired Joyce. She was looking after the horses seven days a week and arranging lessons for all those kids. She had an amazing but hard life at that farm and handled everything with a big smile. On top of all the work she had to do, day in and day out, she also had her ladies. "Well, I have to go now and feed the ladies," she would say and scuttle off. I thought she meant her dogs, until I discovered that there were two old women, even older than Joyce, living with her in the farmhouse. She was collecting money from the government to be their caregiver. She was constantly scraping by and working hard. The first winter I spent at Joyce's was long and harsh; the snow would often come up over her knees as she'd lead horses into the barn. We were worried about everything freezing; the doors didn't close properly and the cold was relentless. It was a hard life for a woman of her age and probably the right time for her to hang up her shovel. But it didn't feel right. She had to quit because of money, and that seemed to me the worst way to make a decision.

I first stood in her driveway the day she went and gave her a hug. She laughed awkwardly, shrugged, like "Oh well," and drove away into a different world.

I waited there for a while, thinking about things. I'd liked my job and it had gone down the driveway too. It seemed like another chapter of my life had ended just when I was getting comfortable. The sun was going down, and as I walked home a familiar blanket of loneliness began falling over me. When I got to my driveway, I hesitated, looking at my farmhouse. I felt small and narrow, and for the first time since moving to Canada I asked myself, "What are you doing here?" I noticed the farmhouse itself looked a little stark and lonely too. That's when I became conscious of the familiar hum—very faint, but the same hum I'd heard sitting in my cramped bedroom in London, waiting for the day to end.

But as I looked at the house, a silver shadow walked out from under a tree. Sonnet. And suddenly I was filled with gratitude. I had bought Sonnet. About a week earlier I had made a quick decision to buy him because he was lame at that moment, and I thought if he went back to the horse dealer, he might end up going for meat. It's a sad truth about the horse industry, but when horses are lame or not useful anymore, they seem to disappear. Some lucky ones end up at rescue facilities and are rehomed, but what often happens is needlessly cruel because of the horse meat industry. Canada is a large supplier of fresh horse meat to different regions, such as Asia, France and even Quebec. Horses are taken to the sales barn, where they are auctioned off and sometimes bought by the meat man. Because Ontario closed its abattoirs, the horses are put on trailers and shipped to Alberta or Quebec, where they are slaughtered, or flown to different countries to be killed for dishes such as sushi or filet chevalin. It's a terrible journey for the horses; they are sometimes without food or water for more than twenty hours, in overcrowded crates. Kind owners euthanize their horses and then send the carcasses to the abattoir, thus saving the horses distress. Some lucky horse owners who have property will bury their horses, but, sadly, most horses end up on the meat wagon.

To make sure Sonnet was safe, I decided to buy him for a thousand dollars, and just like that he was mine. Life had taken another turn and I was following along, watching it unfold. I had moved Sonnet across the road to my paddock, and he shared the field with a Haflinger pony that the farmer owned. After a month or so we found another Appie for my boyfriend, a lovely spotty chestnut called Bucky. Finally my childhood dream of living with my horses had come true. Everything was exciting; even going to the feed store and buying water buckets and halters would fill me with happiness.

That first summer, my boyfriend and I had an amazing time. He was a natural on a horse, and we would go out on evening rides at dusk when he got home from work. The horses were a good team, and we would gallop around and explore all the farmers' fields and vacant land around the back of the property. Our horses gave us a common interest and we enjoyed them together.

As the evenings started drawing in, we had to start planning for the cold winter ahead. We bought heaters for the water troughs that kept them from freezing even when the temperature dipped down to minus twenty-five degrees Celsius. The horses needed warm rugs, good shelter so they could get in from the wind and snow, and a constant supply of hay. Riding in winter was also hard. We had to wait for the perfect kind of cold day when the snow was just right: not so sticky that it would ball up in their hooves, but not so icy that they would slip or fall. I hacked a lot in the winter and found that following the farmers' snowmobile or tractor tracks was the best. Sometimes it felt like riding on sand. Many owners don't tough out the long cold winters; they move their horses to barns with indoor arenas so they can ride inside all winter. We couldn't afford such luxury, so we made do.

Canadian summers can also be tough. It seemed winter had been over for about a week when we suddenly had to deal with horseflies the size of olives and a mess of mosquitoes.

Keeping the horses fed became a large part of my daily life because the dry and often excessive heat made it hard to grow grass. I also had to muck out the fields regularly because it's better for the horses' health—and anyway, who wants to look at a field full of horse poo? The horses had become a part-time job, and they also meant I was tied to the property. I'd been used to freedom, but what with the horse chores and the dog and then cats and chickens, it was like one big slippery animal slope.

It wasn't long before we were altering fence lines and making our world into a horsey dream. This included bringing the back fence line right up to the living room window so we could give the horses carrots at night while we were watching a movie. In the evenings we would often sit on the porch with a glass of wine and watch our Appaloosas grazing in the front paddock as the sun went down. I'd put my feet up and feel very content with my lot. The hustle and bustle of Toronto faded away, except for the tiniest of shimmers on the skyline.

Some horses are the boss; they are the boss in the field, the boss when you are grooming them and the boss when you are on board.

When I would hack Sonnet, he absolutely had to take the lead. The mere hint of him going behind another horse threw him into a tizzy. He would let me know immediately that this was not something he could abide, but always with an eye out for my safety, and that's why we got along. I trusted him because he never unseated me. Anyone else who got on him generally got off pretty quickly because they didn't feel safe. He was what some people call a one-person horse.

When we would hack out on our own, he was perfect. We went out for hours on the beautiful trails through the York Regional Forest, just me and my horse, like companions on a heroic journey. It was a wonderful feeling, the type of feeling they talk about in movies. But every six months or so, he would go lame on those funny front legs of his, and it was starting to get frustrating. When a tendon got sore I'd often have to rest him for three or more months. He hated being off work and would paw at the gate when I took Bucky out instead. At night he'd stand in the middle of the field and look up at the stars, his head tilted in the funniest of ways, as if asking why his life was the way it was. Some call it moon blindness, but I think he was trying to make sense of the world. I've heard that other horses don't like grey or white horses because they stand out at night and give away the herd location in the wild, and I can confirm this is true. Sonnet would shine in the moonlight like a beautiful silver ghost. I always knew where he was.

For the first year, having a horse and living on a farm felt like enough for me. My boyfriend was doing well; his landscaping business had taken off and he got a crew of people. I worked alongside him after Joyce left, and for a while it was good. But as he did better, he became more driven and worked longer hours. He also became more assertive, which was often annoying. All in all, working in Toronto in the hot sun and then looking after the farm was becoming exhausting and putting a strain on our relationship. So when I was asked to produce an album for an up-and-coming songwriter, I jumped at the opportunity, made part of our farmhouse into a recording studio and worked on that for six months. But there are many hours in a day, and having more time on my hands led to my old friend, ambition, showing up and tugging at my toes. I was romanticizing the idea of training again, and looked into taking up the sport of dressage.

Dressage, which is often translated as "training," encompasses the foundations of riding. It goes back to classical Greek horsemanship, when the military trained its horses to perform movements in battle. The aim of modern dressage is to produce a lightness in and command of your mount that gives you a feeling of weightlessness. Dressage has a training scale that should be followed, starting at Training Level, followed by Levels 1 to 4, then Prix St. Georges, two Intermediate levels and finally Grand Prix. I was at about Level 1. As with most competitive sports, once you poke your head down this rabbit hole, you can easily disappear. That's what happened to me; the more I learned about dressage, the more obsessed I became. To train a horse up to the highest level in the sport can take six years or more of full-time training. It's extremely hard, and only a small percentage of horses make it to the top. But training at the lower levels can give you a sense of achievement, which acts like a powerful drug.

I'd done some dressage in England as part of eventing, but the actual sport of dressage was a different beast. It was exhilarating to have a new passion, and I eagerly looked around for a dressage instructor so I could take lessons. I also needed new equipment. I was still riding in the jodhpurs I had brought over from England, which were now twenty years old. I soon discovered many tack shops in my area that were stuffed from floor to ceiling with every horsey thing imaginable. There were rows and rows of breeches, shirts, jackets, boots and helmets. Bridles and saddles stacked high.

Bronze and silver bits, spurs and crisp white saddle pads, all sparkling and new. It was fun, like buying for a child who never says no to anything. As well, each horse was a different size and had different needs, so the tack shops were always busy with all sorts of horsey people, discussing all sorts of horsey needs. I loved going to these stores. I could chat at length with the salesperson about trying a certain supplement or a new bit and while away an hour or so at a place where everyone understood my passion.

Sonnet wasn't built for dressage, although he was so solid in his rhythm that I probably could have done okay at the lowest levels. I never took him to a show—that just wasn't something I wanted to do with him. But as I began taking the odd lesson, thoughts of showing took hold again.

Around the same time, things at the farm got hectic. The owner decided to rent part of the property to someone who was using it to dump fill, so all of a sudden there were twelve-wheeler trucks coming up the driveway every twenty minutes. It was noisy and not at all the atmosphere we wanted to live in, so we decided to look for our own farm and take a leap into commitment. We didn't have much money, but the thought of being able to buy any land at all was very romantic to us. One day when I was out driving with my dad, who was visiting, we saw a property for sale near Uxbridge. It was set on a dirt road in a small valley and gave the impression it hadn't had much love in a while. We stopped the car and had a peek over the fence line, and I smiled at my dad; it was perfect. But as we drove away I felt a shudder go down my spine. The Crow was back; it swooped down and landed on my shoulder. Was I doing the right thing? Was this my future? I shook it off... and watched it fly away.

At dusk that evening I took my boyfriend over to see the farm, and together we trespassed and looked around. The property had obviously been a pig farm at one time and had lots of funny little sheds. It was all overgrown, with old machinery lying about, but it was affordable, and we could see potential in the scrubby fields and the tiny bungalow with its ugly siding. We knew it was in a good location, so we held hands and made a plan.

The next day we made an offer, which was immediately accepted. My father helped us out with the down payment, and we celebrated with a bottle of champagne. One month later we took possession and began the long job of making this farm into our home. We decided to section off one side for my boyfriend's business and a tree nursery, and keep our horses on the other side. We put in a few fences and moved the horses over as soon as we could. It was rustic, to say the least, but it was ours, and it was an exciting time.

I'm sure if you had watched us over our fence line in those first few months, working away, you would have thought we were the perfect couple, but even then we were drifting apart and into our own versions of the truth. Our relationship became project oriented—and was as distant as that sounds. We were great friends but not great lovers, and we both dealt with this on our own. We never talked about it; we just strode on, looking straight ahead. But the conversation in my head was getting louder and my boyfriend was getting quieter. The Crow would sweep down and sit on my shoulders for weeks and then months.

I'd sit in the shadow of its wing.

Should I be here?

I kept Sonnet for about five more years. During this time my boyfriend's young niece Hannah became a frequent visitor to the farm. She learned to ride on Sonnet, which was a little nuts at first, but she was tough as nails and didn't mind his shenanigans. Also, as Sonnet grew older he became kinder and less contentious, and we all loved him. Eventually I gave him to the woman across the road so she could hack him. But one day he arrived back on my doorstep when she told me she couldn't deal with him escaping anymore. He stayed at the farm for a few weeks, but by this time I had other horses and they did not get along. It was sad to watch because he had always been the boss on turnout, and now he was low on the pecking order and being picked on mercilessly. I had to separate him from the others, and he hated being alone, as most horses do. He would race up and down the fence line until he was in a lather, calling for the other horses, day after day. It got to be too much for me, so I advertised him as a companion horse and a week later a nearby horse sanctuary said they could take him. I drove him over and met a sweet woman, reminiscent of Joyce, who was helping rehome horses. She took Sonnet and I made a donation to her cause. She phoned me a week later to let me know that she had found a forever home for Sonnet out in Port Perry with an Appie mare. I smiled; I knew he liked the girls.

Sonnet brought me back into my horse world and made me feel courageous. I loved his spirit and his strength. He was so alive and never compromised his behaviour for anyone. I didn't see him again after the day I took him to the sanctuary. I probably could have, but I didn't even ask where his new home was. I should have made sure he was all right, but I didn't. I handed the woman the lead rope and walked away, even though he was my good friend. I forgot that I loved him. He had been in my life for ten years and we had shared many hours in the woods, where I had never felt closer to a living being. But at that moment I didn't want to look after him; I didn't want the responsibility. I cut my feelings off because I was good at that. I strode away, looking forward, not back.

Because I had a lot on my mind.

I was trying to build a future.

Trying to make a home.
Trying to belong.
Trying to be in love.
Trying to be happy.
Trying the best with what I had available to give.
And living a lie.

CHAPTER 6

Chicky, 2001–2006

I never married my boyfriend. But from the moment we bought our farm together I considered him my husband. So from here on I'll call him that.

People would ask why we hadn't tied the knot, and I had a list of reasons. Like I'm not a believer in having to do paperwork to show togetherness. And why would I want to get married in a church when I'm not religious? Or I'd say it didn't do my parents any good, so what's the point? But the truth is, he never asked, and I'm not sure what I would have said if he had. I didn't know if I could stand at an altar and do the whole vow thing when I lived in so much doubt. But at the same time I wondered what it must feel like to be that much in love. Another part of me fantasized about holding his hand and walking down our dirt road with a stream of friends behind us and having some kind of ceremony to celebrate our life together.

But we never did anything like that. We built fence lines and did renovations.

One of our first big projects was to clear out one of the pig sheds and convert it into a studio for me. It was an awesome rustic space, with an old wood stove and a screen door that looked out onto the horses' field. I did some recording for friends and made a few albums, but my music world was now just a hobby at

Chicky.

best. Without a manager and record company it was hard to get heard in the big sea of borderless music. I was no good at creating opportunity without a team. I was asked to partake in the odd tour, playing music in France, but I stopped getting any decent shows in Canada, and when I stopped playing music, I stopped seeing a lot of my good friends. They all presumed I had become a recluse, but what was happening was that the horse passion was taking over.

To pursue dressage I needed a horse that was better suited to the job. I was very much in love with the heavier type of horse and became aware of the Canadian horse, or *le cheval canadien*. The breed descended from horses imported from France in the 1600s that were given to settlers in Quebec to help with clearing forests and plowing fields. These horses became like members of the farming families because people depended on them for their survival. They were a mix of draft breeds crossed with lighter riding horses, making them short and very stocky; they usually stand around 15 hands and are mostly black, dark bay or chestnut. They are also known as the little iron horse, or *le petit cheval de fer*, because pound for pound they are one of the strongest pulling horses around.

The Canadian horse's history is that of a survivor, but only just. In 1861 when the American Civil War broke out, many Canadian horses were exported to fight as cavalry horses, hauling cannons and taking men into battle. Thousands of horses were sold and exported, and large numbers perished, putting the breed into a decline. There are many amazing stories of these horses saving soldiers' lives and surviving in terrible conditions. The same thing happened when the First World War came along. Then, during the Great Depression, thousands of farming families couldn't find food for themselves or their horses. Sadly, in some cases they had to eat their horses to survive. By mid-century the Canadian horse had almost died out, and in the 1970s there were only about four hundred registered Canadian horses left. Since then, however, their numbers have been slowly increasing.

In 2006, when I told people I wanted to buy a Canadian horse, they would look at me blankly. I thought that was the kind of history all Canadian people would know, yet hardly anyone I talked to had heard of this little iron horse that had pretty much built Canada on its back.

Although a Canadian was not considered a dressage horse, I had no aspirations at that point to get up to the high levels in dressage. I had a lot to learn. With dressage, like many other sports, the basics can take the most time and probably involve the biggest learning curve.

At any rate, I set out to find myself a Canadian, and it didn't take long. By this point the internet had exploded, so, unlike horse shopping when I was a girl in England, there was an incredible catalogue of horses for sale online. Because Canadian horses were relatively rare, I felt lucky to find a mare not too far away, and I went to have a look at her. I didn't want another mare, but she was the only Canadian I could find for sale in Ontario. She was four years old and, typical of the breed, dark bay, 15 hands, no white markings and built like a small tank. There were so few Canadians around that she was being offered for five thousand dollars, which was a high price. But because I was so in love with the breed and the story, I didn't look at any other type of horse. I knew what I wanted and that was that.

As usual, I walked into the situation blinded by what I wanted to see and didn't look at what was right in front of me. She was a stunning mare, and although only four years old, she was very muscular and beefy. When I rode her she was powerful and moved well, but I was disappointed. She didn't excite me, and she was spooky. "Spooky" is a term for a horse that looks at things and gets scared. Horses are flight animals; some of them are very nervous and others not at all. For instance, Sonnet hadn't spooked much the whole time I had him. But this mare was very nervous of her surroundings—so nervous it was hard even riding her around the ring.

When I asked her owners why she looked at everything, they said, "It's probably because she doesn't know you."

I believed them because I wanted to and rode blindly on. I bought her without a second thought because I had already sold myself her story. She was a *canadien* and I was riding her amazing heritage with pride.

This mare's name was Adanac Hope because of her lineage, and her owners had called her Hope for short, which I disliked, so I named her Chicky. I thought it was sweet and suited her. That may have been a mistake; renaming a horse is sometimes considered bad luck.

When I got Chicky home I was gung-ho to start dressage training and booked a lesson with a local dressage trainer called Jane. But Chicky was difficult. She found the far end of any arena full of ghosts and would stop dead to peer at whatever she thought she saw. Because she was a Canadian and very strong, she didn't care what I did to encourage her to go forward and stood stock-still. It was extremely frustrating and made me feel inconsequential and almost stupid. I kept hoping it would be fine because spooky horses are common enough, and they usually become less nervous over time. I just had to be patient. I carried on but with that same nagging feeling I'd had with Woofy. The "surely this will change" feeling.

Despite Chicky's spookiness, I was very excited about my new life at the farm, and having horses again was still a luxury for me. I wanted to try new things, so I began chatting with a couple of cowboys. I call them cowboys because they owned ranches, not farms, and they wore Lariat Stetsons, pointed leather buckaroo boots, wrangler cowboy-cut jeans and button-down shirts all the time. And I mean *all* the time, even to go to the supermarket. Cowboy Jim, who was the older, more experienced cowboy, told me on one occasion that he only ever took his Stetson off to take a shower. He and his young apprentice, Justin, were the trainers people called in when they had a horse that was acting up and they couldn't deal with it themselves. They were two of the best, and only, "horse whisperer"–type trainers in the area, and they happened to live right on my road. They also knew a lot about local horse events and where the good hacking was.

One day Justin mentioned that there was a western gathering every other Thursday night where people did team penning, a sport involving rounding up cows on horseback. He invited my husband and me to tag along. In team penning, you have to round up cattle and drive them into pens. It's fast and fun. I thought this might be good for Chicky because it would perhaps desensitize her and make her more worldly. It was also something I could do with my husband and his horse.

So the next Thursday we hitched a ride with Justin in his horse trailer, and next thing I knew I was sitting on Chicky in a large pen with a bunch of cattle running about. It's fun trying new things, but it was a bit of a disaster. First off, I was concerned for these calves and what they must think of all this chasing, so I tried not to scare them. I was assured that they were looked after like athletes and led exotic lives compared with most cattle, but I felt sorry for them. Chicky was horrified by the whole event, and when it was our turn she stood like a rock and wouldn't budge. When a calf wandered toward us she stood straight up on her hind legs like a grizzly bear and just stayed there. She would come down but go straight back up. Over and over again. It was so embarrassing. Rearing is typically a deal breaker for me—I won't keep a horse that rears—but in this instance I decided to ignore it because rounding up cows was not something Chicky really had to do. From then on she stayed at home and I watched my husband team penning from time to time.

I hung up my Stetson because dressage was calling my name. Like chocolate in the cupboard, it was enticing me. I bought books about balancing your seat and balancing your horse with training exercises, and I watched tutorial videos that I rented from the tack stores. The more I learned, the more I wanted to learn; it was like a drug and I was hooked. I looked forward to my one weekly lesson with Jane so much that it was like being transported back in time to Barwell, getting ready the day before the lesson, cleaning my tack and polishing my boots, with everything laid out and prepared. It wasn't long before I was looking up local dressage groups online and discovering that there were lots of events and clinics in my area. Then one day I responded to an online ad for a working student at a nearby dressage barn. I thought this would be an easy way to dive into the deep end of the sport, and a week later I went for an interview.

The dressage facility I applied to was fancy. It was one of those places where you turn down a driveway not so different from many driveways you've turned down before, then realize you're in a different world. Rolling, manicured, green lawns with vast colour-ful flower beds stretched out beside long rows of immaculate, black wooden post-and-rail fence lines. A massive stone mansion stood at the top of the hill, towering over a giant equestrian palace sprawled out in the valley below; it had turrets and weather vanes and was magnificent. I pulled in and parked my Mazda beside a black Mer-cedes and knocked on the tall wooden door. I was shown in by a very tidy staff member in clean paddock boots and a custom barn jacket, who asked me to wait in an office full of ribbons and trophies.

When the lead trainer (Trainer 1), heiress to this dressage dynasty, walked into the room, the air seemed to change density; she was so impressive that I found it hard to breathe. She strode toward me in a casual T-shirt tucked into gorgeous plaid breeches tucked into stunning navy-blue polished leather dressage boots adorned with large silver spurs. She was tall, slim and very striking. She shook my hand with a firm grip but didn't quite look me in the eye, then swung around and strode off. I followed her as she led me on a tour around the facility.

As we moved through the barn, the staff looked down and busied themselves. We breezed along aisles of elegant, immacu-late stalls with clean new shavings, clean matching water buckets and clean windows for the horses to look out at their clean indi-vidual paddocks. Handsome horses nickered at Trainer 1, and she stopped often to give them mints from her pocket and tell me their names, breeding and showing level. We marched on and on. She waved her hand nonchalantly at things like the tack room, which in all honesty was nicer than my house and had about fifty thousand dollars' worth of saddles in it. She brushed it off like it was aver-age and looked annoyed when she mentioned that it was somewhat cramped. She seemed to feel almost out of place and maybe even embarrassed at all that was hers. She then walked me through huge gleaming wooden doors into an indoor riding arena the size of an aircraft hangar. It had huge walls of windows at each end and mirrors running down the sides, above kickboards that were newly varnished and gleamed in the afternoon light. The footing in the arena had recently been harrowed and, she told me, was made of small pieces of fibre, which was the best footing that money could buy. The grooming area had heated showers, and vacuums for the horses' coats. Everything about the facility was immaculate and impressive, and my cheeks went pink as I looked down at my cheap boots.

Trainer 1 was animated and charming. We talked for a while about the job and what it entailed and then about my horse-riding experience. We also talked about my career as a musician, which she found fascinating, since she loved alternative music. By the end of our conversation I was thinking, "Okay, well, this is going to be an experience." And when she offered me the job, I took it.

I've always been attracted to this particular type of person; I call them room changers—they can immediately change the atmosphere with their energy. All through my life I've gravitated toward these people, comfortably leeching on to and feeding off their aura. I think I'm the perfect sidekick because I'll go along with anything. In my eyes, Trainer 1 was a multimillion-dollar room changer and I was up for the ride.

As a working student I was to arrive before her and get the horses ready for her to train. For that I received a small wage and one lesson a day on one of her horses. It seemed like an okay deal because her lessons were expensive, and getting taught every day was an exciting prospect. But I didn't have a clue as to what I had signed up for. The days were long, and it was hard work. On average, Trainer 1 rode six horses a day and taught three lessons, so I had to motor. The job was meant for eighteen-year-olds who wanted to become dressage professionals. At that time I was thirty-four and just wanted to improve my riding skills. I was going full tilt from 10 a.m. until 4 p.m., and the only time I sat down was when I was riding a horse. I wasn't in the best shape when I started, and I'd go home exhausted every night.

Working in a dressage barn was a steep learning curve for me. I thought I knew a lot, but this was a different world. Every horse had a unique set of rules and requirements; some of them were difficult to deal with, almost to the point of being dangerous, so I had to be careful.

Until that time I had never met or ridden a warmblood, and that was pretty much the only type of horse in her barn. Warmbloods are the result of breeding programs in Europe where they crossed "cold-blooded" horses, such as Percherons and Belgians, with "hot-blooded" horses, such as Arabs and Thoroughbreds. Over the years, and with careful selection, warmbloods were crossed with other warmbloods until they became tantamount to superhorses. They are considered by many to be the Rolls-Royce of horse breeds. There are many types from different areas in Europe, but they mostly hail from Germany and Holland. Warmbloods are expensive, and riding one of these horses comes with a certain amount of pomp. Some warmbloods are branded to show what lineage they are, depending on the specific breed's rules, which is a controversial practice that these owners accept because it sets their horses apart from others.

The first time I rode one of Trainer 1's superhorses, my jaw dropped and I looked at her like she was pulling a joke on me. The power and bouncy stride was crazy, and I could not for the life of me sit the trot. Every bit of pride I had about my riding ability was stripped away from me as I bounced around in the saddle.

Initially, every day seemed like a week, and my life was busy and full. I went from feeling fairly lonely at home most of the day to being surrounded by a lot of excitement, and it was overwhelming at first. I got on well with Trainer 1, though, and as the weeks went by, our friendship grew and we started socializing outside of the barn. We went to tack stores, riding clinics and pubs together, and met each other's partners. We became friends, then best friends, and all of a sudden we were inseparable. It was a little like falling in love. I think she enjoyed hanging around with me because I was a clean slate: I knew nothing about the local dressage scene, none of its players, none of its gossip, nothing. I was working in the boots I'd played gigs in while on tour in Paris. I had no idea about the society I'd just joined and how it would take hold of the next few years of my life.

It took me a while to see the dark side of the setup. Trainer 1 had several students who came in for lessons, and it never occurred to me that a dressage trainer could be worshipped like a rock star. Her power and wealth made the students nervous and awkward. I think their insecurity was mostly because a lot of them had no idea what they were doing; they would wander into the barn in immaculate new riding attire and a brand-new helmet, thinking they could become a good rider overnight. They were like weekend punk rockers, trying to adopt the lifestyle without knowing how to get dirty. We had to be incredibly careful that they didn't get hurt because some of these warmbloods were not for beginners. These rich clients would catch the horse bug and think they could buy their dream. On one occasion one of them confided that she had asked Trainer 1 to go to Europe and bring her back a black stallion because she wanted to buy a horse the same colour as her sports car. So Trainer 1 shrugged her shoulders and went to Germany, bringing back a beautiful four-year-old black warmblood. The client had a couple of lessons on her stunning new steed, got terrified and asked to be put back on one of the older school horses. Trainer 1 then suggested to the client that she train the nice new horse herself, ostensibly to school it so it would be more "rideable" for the amateur owner to manage. But I was told that what usually happened in situations like this was that Trainer 1 would end up showing the new horse, and its owner would never have the chops to get back on her black beauty. What shocked me, after watching this chain of events, was the conversations behind the client's back as Trainer 1 and other clients made fun of the situation. I'd laugh awkwardly and shake my head at all the right moments, then walk away feeling embarrassed and ashamed. I hadn't been involved in anything like this since my school days. I tried to stand back and watch, but before long I got sucked into the conversation, even though it made me feel dirty. I'd get home in the evenings and feel like I was part of something bad. As time went on, though, my grasp on reality faded; I became a disciple of the barn and the backstabbing culture. I'd eat, drink and sleep my new life. I got to know all the players and formed my own outspoken opinions. I became one of them.

After six months, Trainer 1 began putting me on more of her horses, and my riding started to take shape. I even had the opportunity to ride an older Grand Prix horse, which meant he was at the highest level you can go to in dressage—Olympic level. This was an amazing experience; I got to try things that you simply can't do on most horses, like canter pirouettes, passage, which looks like the horse is trotting in slow motion, and one-tempi changes, where a horse is literally skipping. But the lessons were gruelling. It looks easy when you see the pros ride, but I found it extremely hard. I was not blessed with the ideal riding conformation for dressage. It's best to have a short torso, long legs and flexibility; I have a short, tight, narrow body, better suited to…playing the guitar. The lessons were also mind-blowingly repetitive. We would go in circles with constant instruction, pushing and pulling in a particular way, over and over, that would eventually, if you were extremely lucky, enable the horse to go "through"—a term for getting impulsion from the hindquarters that pushes through the body to the front end, lifting the back and dropping the head. The only thing I can liken it to is runner's high, where you feel like you are in ecstasy and almost flying, and everything becomes easier. It's the dressage rider's goal, and in the year and a half that I was riding circles with Trainer 1, I only managed to attain it twice.

The training was intense for the horses too, and they often struggled. Saddles were altered, teeth were rasped, hooves were trimmed, bits were swapped out, even the thickness of a saddle pad was examined and talked about. No expense was spared, but sometimes the horses still said no. This created a lot of frustration, and at times it was hard to watch.

One of my tasks each week was to help with the breeding program, which involved artificial insemination. They had a breeding stallion at the barn, a tall, black, shiny, sleek amalgamation of lean, coiled muscles. On normal days he was training in dressage, but he wasn't doing too well, probably because he spent practically all his energy trying to kill us. He would constantly try to devour me as I was tacking him up. He would turn his big beautiful head toward me and lunge, his teeth bared and ears pinned. It was terrifying. Leading him from his stall to the cross ties would fill me with dread. I'd ignore him and walk with purpose, hearing the gnashing of his teeth beside me. He was like a dragon—a beautiful, black, aggressive, fire-breathing beast.

The stallion was a problem for all the barn staff; we hated dealing with him and complained regularly. Trainer 1 sighed at our incompetence, but we could tell she wasn't that fond of handling him either. After a particularly bad day, which involved the barn manager getting pinned to the gate of the paddock, Trainer 1 arranged for an experienced German dressage rider to come in and show us how to take control of the situation. The German strode into the barn a week or so later, looked at all us horsey women, shrugged and led the stallion into the arena with a nonchalant swagger. He was leading the stallion around, gesturing and talking to us about mindfulness and body language, when the stallion slid to a halt, grew about four inches and snorted like a rhinoceros. The German stopped talking and slowly turned around, and they stood staring at each other as the stallion pinned his ears and rolled back his lips. The German looked a little less plucky as the stallion raised his head even higher. Then the German took a tiny step back—and in one swift blur of intent the stallion charged him. The German leaped to the side like a matador, barely managing to get out of the path of the charging beast. By this point we were grabbing lunge whips and running into the ring. It took some noise and frantic waving, but we kept the stallion away from the German, and we all got out alive. Trainer 1 then gave the stallion some grain, and he looked very happy with himself. The German was furious and shook his head, eyeing us with disgust. He said it was all our fault; we had spoiled the horse and "now he is dangerous." It was a dramatic scene, which ended with the door slamming as he marched away, but I think he knew he had lost when he took that one step back. He had done exactly what he had lectured us on not doing. Never show weakness—and stepping back is a sign of submission. The black stallion had won another day.

Once every two weeks the stallion would be taken to the collection shed, a small barn at the back of the property with a breeding dummy in it. This is a contraption that couldn't be less romantic, a large metal cylinder wrapped in foam, standing about 15.2 hands high, with a single important hole at one end. We would lead him from the barn on that particular trail to the breeding shed, and he would lose his mind. He'd scream, prance and roll his eyes, and it was almost impossible to hold him. Eventually, Trainer 1 decided the safest place to be was on his back and she'd ride him to the breeding shed. When they entered, she'd jump off as he mounted the dummy mare and, well, it was all too much for me and I'd feel faint. Then the semen would be put in a box, frozen and flown to whomever had ordered it.

Breeding afternoon was always a huge event. We would roll up our sleeves and prepare for mayhem. I have to give it to Trainer 1, though; she had guts. Once, she didn't manage to jump off in time and actually sat on him for the act. There's nothing more I can say about that.

After work I would go home and try to find the energy to ride Chicky. She didn't seem to be getting any less spooky, even as my riding got much better. It was frustrating. After hearing me moan about it at work one day, Trainer 1 suggested I bring her in for a few weeks of lessons. I think she believed she could sort Chicky out, but she had the same problems I did. After two weeks of solid schooling, we managed to get Chicky down to the far end of the arena, so Trainer 1 suggested I keep her at the barn, and we could use her in lessons for some of the clients who couldn't manage the big warmbloods. She then suggested I ride one of her younger horses and get her ready to show that summer. This meant that Chicky had a job, which was good, and I got to ride this fancy little warmblood every day. It seemed to be a fantastic opportunity, but it led to many problems, and the energy in the barn began to shift.

When I was working on Chicky, although it was difficult, she was mine. We were going somewhere together. I had my own journey set out. Riding someone else's horse, especially my boss's horse, didn't feel as free because I had to rise up to the trainer's goals for her horse. It became a burden, like working when the supervisor is watching over you, and for some reason you start doing everything wrong. It wasn't surprising, really. Trainer 1 loved her horses, and the fancy little warmblood she gave me to ride was probably worth a small fortune. I began to tiptoe around Trainer 1, afraid of making a mistake and losing her approval. In turn, she started getting annoyed with me over small things. We began making comments under our breath, and then to other people in the barn. Our relationship was sinking, the honeymoon over.

Then one morning I came in to work and a rich client was riding the fancy little warmblood. The barn manager told me that the rich client was a potential buyer and would be showing the fancy little warmblood from then on. I'd lost the ride. I pretended to shrug it off and smiled like I understood, but it stung. I had been so excited about the upcoming show season. I'd bought a new jacket and was getting prepared. It felt nasty, especially that Trainer 1 hadn't talked to me about the change herself. So I got angry, put my head down and just did my job, spending as much time as I could out of Trainer 1's view.

All the grooming and high living had done Chicky some good. She stood in the cross ties in that million-dollar barn and looked like she now fit in. I thought to myself, "I don't need the fancy warmblood. Look at this fantastic Canadian horse." And I took all my acquired knowledge and threw my energy into riding Chicky each evening after work. But I still couldn't get her around the property without a fight; she was suspicious of everything. For instance, she would stop dead and stare at a wheelbarrow like it was a wild animal about to leap at her, even if she had seen it the day before.

One day when I was schooling her, the vet came into the arena to look at another client's horse. We were at the far end of the arena, and Chicky was spooking because someone had left their jacket lying on the kickboards. The vet watched me for a while and then asked if she could give Chicky an eye exam. We took her into the barn, and when the vet shone a light into each eye, she discovered that the cells at the back of the eye were only one colour. Normally a horse has the colours of a rainbow, like an oil slick. The vet wondered if that meant Chicky was finding it hard to see colour, depth and perspective. She said that the Canadian breed's gene pool had been diminished over the years to the point that they often suffered from eye problems.

And there it was. This explanation made perfect sense. It wasn't that Chicky was afraid of everything; she couldn't see properly, and that was what made her so spooky. It was helpful and validating but sad to hear. There is no cure for bad eyesight in horses, so there was nothing I could do. When I bought Chicky, I hadn't thought about having her vetted. It hadn't even crossed my mind, which was a shame because this was something a vet would have spotted. Often when mares don't fulfill their owner's plans, or have health problems, they can become broodmares and you at least get a foal out of a situation like this. But the vet warned me that I shouldn't breed her because eye problems are usually hereditary and it might get passed down to her offspring.

So I took Chicky home.

I still rode her most days after work, hoping I could somehow turn the story around, that one day I would get on and she would trust me. I'd heard of horses with only one eye who were fine, but this was a different problem; Chicky was never able to trust my eyes to guide her. It would be nice to write that I felt sorry for her because it wasn't her fault, but a large part of me was angry that the breeders had sold me a horse with problems for a large sum of money. I tried contacting them but they didn't respond, so I was stuck with her. I kept her for another year and tried to find something she was good at, but in the end I decided to cut my losses and sell her. This was difficult, because I couldn't lie about her spookiness, and the type of adult amateur who would want a Canadian horse would probably not be interested in a horse with bad eyesight. I also knew she wouldn't pass a vetting. I put her price down to half what I had paid for her, but I still couldn't find a buyer so I ended up swapping her for another horse that I eventually gave away.

I know it sounds mean, but I wasn't too sad to see her go. When you do everything for your horse and spend so much time and money, you feel like you at least deserve to enjoy riding her. The hours and hours I'd put in were in vain. She represented failure to me—my own failure, yet again, to be careful when making an important decision like buying a horse. She also represented misplaced trust. If you've ever been taken advantage of, you'll know the feeling of annoyance that can hound you.

The woman I gave Chicky to only wanted to hack her, and I hoped that if she was following another horse through the woods, she would be okay with that.

So I said goodbye and walked away.

When I saw you
I didn't see you
I saw the history
That's in you
I didn't look
In your eye.

When you saw me
You didn't see me
You saw an outline
Coming at you
Strange monster
In black and white.

One leg at each corner
Like a building
You stood
And waited
For me
To stop pressure
And go
Our separate ways.

CHAPTER 7

Ollie (Orca), 2003–2011

I suppose it speaks to my rebellious spirit, but I still wanted to find a heavier type of horse to join me on my dressage journey. I had a thing for the bigger horses, and there were a few large draft crosses that managed to reach the top of the dressage show ladder, so I knew it could be done. Looking out into the dressage world, you could see it was probably a one-to-thirty ratio of other types of horses to the warmbloods, but in my underdog way I didn't mind these odds, and I also didn't have the money to buy a warmblood. I wanted a horse that was different, a statement.

Some horses just catch your eye. When I saw Ollie's photo in an online ad, I gasped. He was magnificent. I immediately wanted to go and try him. He was a 16.1-hand Percheron–American Paint cross gelding and a perfect symmetrical example of black-and-white beauty.

The Percheron is my favourite of the draft horse breeds. Percherons originated in France and were initially used as war horses. Later they pulled carriages and did farm work, but they are one of the few draft breeds also considered a good English riding horse. Their numbers declined rapidly during the world wars, when they were used for pulling cannons and making railroads, but they survived. If you cross a Percheron with a lighter breed, such as a Thoroughbred, you can get a very agile but

Ollie after a roll in his paddock.

heavier sport horse. I love the way they move and the roundness of their conformation.

Ollie had had a difficult start in life because he was a product of the pregnant mare urine (PMU) industry in western Canada. PMU ranches take draft mares, impregnate them with semen from smaller Thoroughbred stallions, then extract the estrogen from their pee while they are pregnant. The estrogen is used in hormone replacement therapy for menopausal women. The gestation period for a mare is twelve months, so that's a lot of pee. I'm sure it was a harsh life for the mares, and when they had their babies, the youngsters were often slaughtered at birth or set free to run wild on the prairie or in large pastures. At the age of two or three they were rounded up by the PMU ranchers and sold off either as riding horses or, sadly, for meat. Growing up, the young colts and fillies didn't see many humans, so they were not well socialized with people. It was a huge industry, with almost five hundred ranches in North America at its height in the early 1990s. As a result, many draft-cross horses ended up in the marketplace in Ontario.

Ollie had been a PMU problem child. He was originally bought, sight unseen, at an online horse sale and shipped from Alberta. He didn't settle in at his new barn and was apparently acting in a very aggressive manner. The woman who had bought him decided, after a few horrible experiences, to sell him at the local horse market because she was too afraid to go near him. Luckily for Ollie, a man called Blacksmith John, a lead huntsman and farrier, spotted him and saved him from the meat man. As soon as Blacksmith John got Ollie home, he noticed that Ollie's behaviour was particularly stud-like, so he asked his vet to make sure Ollie had been gelded properly. In his words, they "flipped Ollie over" and found that he still had one testicle sitting high and out of view. They removed it, and he said Ollie was a different horse the very next day. When a horse is a "rig," or "ridgling," it means that his testicles may not have descended properly, and therefore he was not gelded properly. This can throw a horse's testosterone way out of whack and, as hard as a stallion can be to manage, a rig can be far worse.

By this time Ollie had been pushed around and beaten into submission many times, which must have been ugly with a horse his size. However, Blacksmith John was good with Ollie and brought him along slowly, eventually taking him field hunting, where apparently Ollie stole the show. He was such a spectacular mover that the whole field would stop to watch him prance along. Blacksmith John had never had a horse that moved the way this horse did, and he decided that maybe Ollie was too fancy for field hunting and put him up for sale, hoping someone would see his potential. When I went to try Ollie out, he had never done an ounce of dressage but was fit and well-behaved.

It was winter and a nasty windy evening when I set out with Trainer 1 to see Ollie. We had arranged to meet Blacksmith John at a barn near Palgrave, about halfway between our farms. When we walked into the arena, this huge, dazzling, black-and-white horse was standing like a rock in the middle of the ring. He was gorgeous, but I was taken aback by how massive he was, like a heavy-set man. As I ran my hand down his neck and his huge thick legs, I thought maybe I had made a mistake. He stood like a statue, his eyes focused straight ahead, his head up high. He was so alert, taking everything in as the fabric of the arena's roof and walls groaned and flapped in the cold winter wind. Horses give off an energy, and Ollie's was that of a general who had lost some battles.

Blacksmith John got on him and walked him around the ring once each way, then trotted forward. That's when Trainer 1 and I glanced at each other and smiled. Ollie looked like he was floating slightly above the ground, and a part of me was sold on him at that point. Blacksmith John then stopped, jumped off and said to Trainer 1, "You're the expert," and handed her the reins. Trainer 1 was clearly excited, though she commented that it might look ugly when she rode him because she would try to get him to go on the bit. This meant she would try to get him to accept connection from her hands and legs. She popped on and it didn't look ugly at all. She gave him a good schooling, pushing him to see how he would react. By the time she got off there was steam coming up from his back, so when I got on I only rode a few circles, but I was in awe. He was light on his feet, but at the same time so strong it made me feel uneasy, like he was a cat waiting to pounce.

Trainer 1 really liked Ollie and said he moved like a warmblood, which is what you want to hear. She thought I should buy him, but a part of me felt anxious and was concerned that maybe he was too much horse for me, so I asked if I could try him once more.

The following week I drove to Blacksmith John's farm. It was a nice old place south of Orangeville, with a lovely big barn that loomed over the paddocks like a cathedral. Horses were munching on hay in some of the paddocks, and there, tied to a fence, was Ollie, looking like a giant chess piece. He took my breath away again, but I also had that familiar sense of dread knocking at my temples. I had to talk myself into getting on. When I did, I had the same feeling as before, that he wasn't relaxed and was just containing himself. I didn't tell Blacksmith John any of this, so when he suggested I take Ollie into a field to round up some cows, I nodded like it wasn't a big deal. But, bloody hell, I was in knots inside! I gathered up the reins and walked him forward.

As we entered the cow field, Ollie tensed up underneath me, and he seemed to grow a couple of inches taller. I held the reins a little tighter but he kept it together and floated across the puddles with his huge stride. Blacksmith John joined me on another horse, and we rounded up and moved the cows around the field, which was captivating and kind of like grabbing a hockey stick when you can't skate. It took my focus off Ollie and I relaxed. Ollie had immense power, like a ride at the fairground. He was strong and in charge, and he didn't do anything wrong. But as I drove home I couldn't shake the fact that I was nervous, and my mind began circling over and over in a loop, wondering if I was doing the right thing.

Suddenly the Crow swooped down and sat on my shoulder. I hadn't had the Crow visit for a long time, and I didn't like it. It was restless, and its squawking kept me up that night. It was hard to ignore, but I tried because I really wanted this horse. The next day Trainer 1 suggested that I ask if I could take Ollie on a two-week trial. This is a smart thing to do whenever you're buying a horse, and until that moment I hadn't even known it was an option.

Later that week Blacksmith John dropped Ollie off at Trainer 1's barn. When Ollie stepped off the trailer, he was nervous and skittish. It worried me how stressed he was: his head high, his neck tight. It's fairly normal for a horse to be on edge when you take him somewhere new, but he was so huge that it felt loaded. I tried to ignore it because, again, he did nothing wrong and he held it together. After a few days he settled in and relaxed somewhat. He was well-mannered through the trial period, so I put in an offer which Blacksmith John accepted.

This time I got my prospective horse vetted. Vetting a horse is like getting a car safety-checked before you buy it. The vet inspects the heart, breathing, eyes and soundness, and gives the horse a close examination. If you are dealing with an expensive horse, you may go one step further and have leg and back X-rays done. Some people even order ultrasounds in certain areas. It is nearly impossible for a horse to pass a vetting with no faults. The vets can always find something, and then another round of price negotiations usually begins. Ollie had a very slight case of ringbone, which is more common in draft-type horses. My vet said she didn't think it would cause trouble but suggested that I knock the price down, just in case. So I negotiated with Blacksmith John and bought Ollie the next day.

I was really excited; this incredible creature was mine. I cleaned him up, pulled his mane and trimmed his fetlocks. He looked magnificent and I was ready to start my training. Things were going well, but the following week something frightened Ollie and he took off with me across the arena. The next day he did it again, and before I knew it the Crow was with me all the time. It spread its wings and was blotting out all my sun. Day after day, Ollie kept charging off with me, to the point where I got too nervous to ride him. Trainer 1 would get on him and look at me and say, "He's fine when I ride him," which was not helpful, but I could see he was nervous even with her.

I took to lunging him with side reins, which allowed me to control his taking off because they kept his head down. When horses bolt, they usually put their heads up in the air and go straight ahead, and it's hard to hang on to them. Every few days I'd get back on and hope he would be over whatever was making him take off. He would be fine for a few minutes. Then he would seem to catch sight of something or his own reflection in the glass, freeze, swing around and gallop to the other end of the arena. And it was a big arena. If he froze for long enough, I'd give him a pat and tell him it was okay, and then he would shoot off, like I wasn't even on board. My nerves were in tatters. It was so upsetting. I had just wanted things to go right after my experience with Chicky. I'd go home in tears.

After a while I noticed it only happened in the indoor arena, so I went out hacking to see if that would ease his nerves. Riding outside was much better—until one day. The day I almost died.

I was riding up a path near the barn. As we rounded the corner, I noticed a hay elevator ahead of us on the path. It stood about twenty feet high and looked like a brontosaurus. Ollie stopped dead, his head shooting up, his heart beating through the saddle. I put my reins in one hand and patted his neck, saying to him, "It's okay, Ollie, it's just a—" and then he went. Suddenly we were galloping through the field to our left. Shooting through thick high grass like a firework gone astray. Up ahead was a huge tree that had fallen on its side, its trunk about four feet high. I pulled hard, turning his head to one side so he wasn't galloping straight at it because I certainly didn't want to jump it. I used the tree to slow him down and he finally came to a stop.

I was shaking. He stood very still and then blew out of his nose like he was now the brontosaurus. I turned him in a few small circles because bending a horse can sometimes help break their flight instinct and lower their adrenaline. I thought about dismounting, but if he took off again with me leading him, I'd lose my horse and who knows where he would end up. It was a Pony Club rule: never get off.

When he calmed down we turned and walked back through the long grass. It was only then that I noticed some old farm equipment lying on the ground in the field—a plow blade and a few sets of harrows, all hidden in the long grass. By some miracle we had managed to dodge them all. A chill ran slowly down my spine. Either he had seen them and was clever enough to not tread on them, or we had been extraordinarily lucky. My mind was painting some horrific pictures, and then I started to laugh out loud. It was a moment of clarity. I didn't walk Ollie past the hay elevator. I went the long way home, but I gained a kind of freedom that day, like I had cheated the grim reaper. I brushed the Crow off my shoulder and told it to get lost. I was going to figure things out because it obviously wasn't my time to die—I was alive.

In the weeks that followed, I played detective to try to understand why my horse was so nervous. I figured part of the problem was that when he was turned out, he was in a field on his own. Maybe he needed a friend. Horses are herd animals; some don't adapt well to being alone all the time, and it can cause behaviour issues. I had to be careful which horse I turned him out with. Because Ollie had been a rig, he might be aggressive, so I looked around for a passive gelding. One of the women at the barn assured me her horse was great with others, so I tried putting them out together. They immediately attacked each other, which was horrific. Horses scream when they fight, and they go at each other like pit bulls. They kick, strike and bite with no mercy. You see the wild animal in them break free as their survival instincts kick in. Luckily they didn't hurt each other, but it was terrifying. After various meetings over the fence with other horses, we found a sweet older gelding for him to go out with. They were a match made in heaven, and Ollie loved him. Slowly his energy changed, and he looked happier. But he was still very nervous when I was riding him.

One day after a particularly bad spook, I phoned Blacksmith John and asked if I was missing something. He certainly knew Ollie better than we did, and I was hoping he might have some suggestions for me. He said, "Oh, he's just taking over. Give him a wallop next time and he'll be fine." I put down the phone, shaking my head. I couldn't imagine giving Ollie a wallop with a whip. It was the total opposite to what my body and instincts were telling me to do. But the next time he froze, I held my breath and smacked him, fast and hard. It was a terrifying moment, but he immediately trotted forward like he understood, cool as a cucumber. I was amazed. A few days later he froze again. I smacked him straight away and the same thing happened: he trotted forward and handed me the keys, and I was now in the driver's seat. Just like that!

I supposed that he had needed me to take charge and assure him that things were safe. Even though he was this huge, striking horse, he wanted me to be boss. I exhaled. After that, everything changed. My confidence returned and I could enjoy my training. I got excited about our future together and breathed a huge sigh of relief.

During this time I was still working for Trainer 1, but our friendship was deteriorating. Gravity had finally taken hold and we were falling fast. I was dragging myself to work each morning with a certain amount of foreboding. We were at that point in the relationship where you notice the way someone chews their cereal. We simply didn't like each other anymore. I'm sure being extremely rich and being treated like a demigod has its own psychological burdens. There must be a lot of pressure to achieve results when your parents have backed your multimillion-dollar lifestyle and sit at the top of the hill in their large mansion, watching over you. But the barn seemed to be sinking beneath the surface of a toxic wave. I hadn't seen anything like this during my musician years, and it brought out a side of me that was disappointing. I couldn't help but chit-chat with the clients about their frustrations with Trainer 1. It was like being back at school and I hated it.

As time went on I stood up for some of the clients when I thought things weren't fair. I stepped in when they needed help, which sometimes took me away from my duties, and Trainer 1 didn't like that. The atmosphere got more and more tense; people were going quiet when I entered the tack room, and I moved through the day with my head down, waiting for the axe to fall.

One morning she walked past me and said, "Outside now." I followed her, bracing myself. I was on her turf—her barn, with her horses, her rules—so I knew how it was going to go. She laid into me like a butcher at Thanksgiving, and I had to concede that some of what she said was accurate. There are always two sides to every story, and I was thinking of backing off until she said, "I thought I was giving you the opportunity to ride a horse you would never be able to afford." My neck stiffened. My eyes bounced up and I looked directly at her. I could see she knew how awful that sounded and that she had gone too far. Suddenly my mother and my father were standing on each side of the gateway to my brain, both carrying swords. I didn't step back. I shrugged like it was nothing and said, "It's okay. I'll go," I walked straight past her, through the barn and out the big wooden doors.

That evening I drove back with my horse trailer to pick up Ollie. I knew Trainer 1 wouldn't be there, so I took my time and said good-bye to all the horses I'd helped look after. I packed all my stuff into a trunk and finished cleaning the bridles that were left hanging on the hook in the tack room. This barn had been my second home for almost two years, and I had seen so much. The staff member who was working that night came and gave me a hug, and I may have wiped away a tear or two. We didn't say much. She walked me out and helped me put Ollie on the trailer, and then I sat in the truck for a few seconds, looking at the beautiful manicured gardens. I wasn't the first or the last person to walk their horse out of those doors under the blanket of twilight, but it felt like I was. I drove away.

A few years before this, I had set up a company called Kurboom Freestyle Music Design. It all started after I went to a dressage show with a friend to watch the kurs, or musical freestyles. This is part of a dressage competition kind of like ice dancing, when horses perform a choreographed test to music. It's a fun event, as riders get to choose their own music, and the horses seem to be dancing through their routines.

As I was watching, I heard some problems with the sound editing: some levels weren't balanced, some of the edits were clumsy and one person's CD skipped. Because of my background in music and my new love for dressage, I decided that maybe I could make these two worlds collide. I stuck up some notices in tack stores and put a few messages in chat rooms online and got my first client. Then came the problem: I really had no idea what I was doing, so I asked for a video of her riding the test and simply spliced the music underneath it, much like adding music to a film. It was difficult because these were still early days for video- and music-editing software, so all I could think of doing was getting an old TV and VHS machine and putting them beside my computer on the desk in my studio. I had to manually sync up the music to keep with the film. There was a lot of stopping and starting, but everything went okay and my first client was happy.

My second client was a game changer. She was one of the top riders in Canada and knew exactly what she wanted. She waltzed into my studio and taught me the ins and outs of this art form. Over the next few years we worked on several of her kurs and became friends. She was the most goal-driven, determined person I have ever met, and she said many times that I could come and train with her if things weren't working out for me where I was. I wasn't sure if she was serious, but I called her on that fateful day when I picked up Ollie, and told her what was going on. She said, "Come on over."

Trainer 2 took me under her wing, and I had almost no time to lick my wounds as I entered a new barn and a whole new level of elite dressage. This was the big leagues, the World Equestrian Games, Pan American Games and Olympic Games. Suddenly, I was standing shoulder to shoulder with Canadian dressage royalty, and it took me a while to notice that my knees were shaking. Trainer 2 had a booming, infectious personality, and you definitely knew who was in charge when you walked into the barn. Like Trainer 1, she could change the air in a room, but it was an even bigger room, maybe a stadium. She was also tall and striking but less flashy. Her breeches were plain blue and her boots traditional black. She was definitely a rock star, but I'd say her music was more alternative, and her riding had a slightly renegade quality. It was her way and it worked. She was one of the most natural riders I have ever trained with. If she got on your horse for ten minutes, it felt like a completely different animal when she handed you back the reins. Like their backs had changed shape. Horses loved her huge, fun personality and tried their hardest for her. She knew how to get them to dance, and I saw comparatively few fights. She had a gift.

Over the years, I worked on some very creative collaborations with Trainer 2 for her dressage freestyles. She was the only rider who commissioned me to create original scores, where I got to employ other musicians and build her music from scratch. One day while we were having tea and talking about her routine, I mentioned that if she ever wanted me to sing live while she was riding, I could. She went still for about one second and then said, "Let's do it at the Royal." My mouth dropped open. The Royal Agricultural Winter Fair is a huge indoor event in Toronto every November, where they show cattle and other livestock, and have a hall full of vendors. They also have a big stadium where they hold a horse show. It's one of the highlights of the Canadian horse world calendar; riders and owners from all the horse disciplines meet up to watch the different horse competitions, drink wine and eat all sorts of food, including a famous fudge. To do anything at the Royal was a huge thrill. A week later I was standing in a red ball gown in the middle of that huge stadium, singing "Hallelujah" to twelve thousand horse fans as Trainer 2 and her beautiful white horse passaged around me. All I could hear as I walked into the centre of the ring was his breath as his hooves danced in perfect rhythm to the music. It was a high point in my horse life. Not many people except Trainer 2 could carry off this kind of plan.

Trainer 2 traded lessons with me for music editing, which was a great deal because I could never have afforded her training otherwise. I only took one official lesson a week, while others rode in full training with her every day. Because we all rode in the same arena, I always thought she was watching over me, and a passing comment could go a long way. As well, the riders formed a close-knit community. We all watched each other and learned from what Trainer 2 would work on with other people. It was intense and wonderfully overwhelming, and I quickly confused my hobby with her other students' dreams. I began to take my dressage very seriously. And then way too seriously. It was a complete lifestyle, like being back at Pony Club camp every day, and for a while I loved it. I had barely any time to think about much else as I buried my head deep in dressage society. In the evenings, my husband would look at me blankly while I went on and on and on and on about horses.

Overnight I was indoctrinated into another group of horsey women. They were a mixed bunch; some were loyal older riders who had been training with Trainer 2 for a decade, while others were younger, competitive riders who were vying to be on Canadian teams. These clients were rich and connected, and knew how to wear their fancy breeches. They worked hard and would all arrive at the barn after lunch, five days a week, and give 100 percent. It was a world of horse competition, horse politics and horse chit-chat. Along with all the training, it was a great social scene, with tons of barbecues and parties. Everyone was welcoming. I made some new friends and soaked up as much information as I could. I got myself some of those fancy breeches and tried my best to fit in.

The riding facility that we trained out of was massive and looked like it had been cobbled together over the years with no particular layout in mind. It had three large indoor arenas, four outdoor rings, and stalls for about seventy horses. Each year it held many shows and events for all the different equestrian disciplines, as well as running a riding school. It was always bustling with activity and constantly changing management and staff, which kept the chit-chat churning because our horses were like gold to us, and we worried about their care. Other dressage instructors taught there, which led to some tension. Sometimes we would all be training in the same arena, and you couldn't help listening in on their lessons. Then the gossip would fly. Horses would change riders, riders would change trainers, trainers would change owners and horses would go lame. It's easy, and very human, to become over-emotional when you are so passionate about your dream. Everyone was talking about everyone; it was a culture of gossip, and again I joined in and didn't like myself for it.

Things would get way too loaded, and feelings got hurt. We all wanted a lot of attention from Trainer 2, but she was teaching all of us and had her own goals to take care of. After a while it was like I was in a relationship that was turning sour. Not my relationship with Trainer 2—we always got along okay—but my relationship with the elite dressage world, a world of money, beautiful people, warmbloods, and winters in Florida, all at a pace I couldn't keep up with. I was starting to get dressage fever burnout and needed to slow it down. My solution was to go hacking more often in the York Regional Forest, and I found that my dressage training actually improved when I wasn't so fixated on it. Ollie loved the woods, and my love of trail riding returned.

I still worked hard with Trainer 2, though, and she spent many hours helping me. She never turned her nose up at Ollie's big chunky self, and after a year or so we were participating in gold-level dressage shows. These are big events where you take your horse for three days and ride your level of dressage test. A dressage test is like a short riding exam. Riders must guide their horses through a set series of compulsory movements and gaits for a judge. These tests indicate whether your horse is competent at a certain level and able to perform the movements. Horses are also marked on quality of gaits, accuracy, freedom, suppleness and more. Riders are judged on their position and effectiveness in the saddle. In Canada there are three levels of showing: gold shows are the highest level, where you really get to strut your stuff. It's expensive, and like any other horse sport there is a "costume" involved: white breeches, show shirt, jacket, white gloves, hairnet, helmet, cravat and these incredibly tall, stiff, black leather boots that sit so high on your legs you can barely sit down to pee.

When I got involved with this higher echelon of dressage, I was encouraged to show gold because I was training in that circle, but it made no sense for an amateur like me. I would be competing against bred-to-win horses that had been imported from Europe and riders from whom I would gladly have taken a lesson. But I also knew that Ollie was impressive and had some genuine qualities, so I gave it a go. What happened was pleasantly surprising: I held my own. It was kind of like performing on stage at a concert. There was a lot of preparation and pomp, but the difference between a dressage test and a gig was the amount of effort versus the amount of time on that stage. A dressage test was about six minutes. It was a great deal of work for basically one song and one audience member—who had a score sheet. Sometimes the judges were kind, but other times it was hard. The comments on that score sheet could be negative, and I would think, "Blimey. I just worked my ass off and spent a crapload of money to be told I'm rubbish." It was like some of the judges were from an era where they needed to show you who was boss in that good old British "let's not mince words" kind of way. I'd get enormously offended, which was all part of the day. I saw many squabbles between riders and judges over the years. It was like a mini soap opera. I tried to ignore it and focus on my riding, and Ollie tried hard, and because I was in full control of my horse, we got to the point where I was riding a pretty accurate and decent test. It didn't matter to me that we usually lost; it mattered that we did our best in the ring. Or that's what I told myself.

As we got up to Level 3, we were working hard five days a week. Ollie was on all sorts of supplements and regimens, and my scores went up into the mid-60s, which is very decent at that level. But it was exhausting and took every ounce of my energy because Ollie was a big, tough horse to ride. They say in dressage that if you have a hundred-thousand-dollar horse, you start at a hundred and lose marks during your test, and if you have a five-thousand-dollar horse, you start from zero and have to earn every point. I didn't mind this scenario; it made me work harder. I held my head up high, riding my huge black-and-white horse, and I gave him a name the judges wouldn't forget: Orca. As I came down centre line to start my test, I would often hear the judge laughing, and I'd smile because I was proud of my killer whale and knew that he was special.

Even though I was welcomed into Trainer 2's orbit, part of me always felt like the fat kid on the scruffy pony. My husband's business was doing well, and we had enough money for me to board Ollie and take the one lesson each week, but it was still expensive. At this point my horses were starting to overlap; I still had Chicky and Sonnet back at my farm, eating their weight in hay each month. I tried to make enough money from Kurboom to pay my horse bills, but editing jobs were sporadic. My horse life and my money balance were off-kilter.

Often ideas happen only when an opportunity gives them to you, and I was at the dressage barn one day when a friend said she had heard of an equestrian facility close by that was available for rent. My engines started turning. Maybe if I ran my own facility, I could pay for all my horses and make a job for myself. I could make money with my hobby instead of just spending it. Perfect.

When I investigated the facility, I discovered it was cheap to rent and full of possibilities, with about twenty stalls, ten paddocks and an indoor arena. It was big enough that I could make some money boarding other people's horses but not so big that I would need to hire a lot of staff to help run it. With my typical head-first jump I signed a lease, then moved my horses in a couple of weeks later. I named it Kingfisher, advertised, and over the next few months got a collection of boarders from many different horse disciplines. My hope was to also find students who wanted to learn the basics of riding and low-level dressage.

Until this point I had no idea what cost and commitment was involved in the day-to-day running of a barn. It was gruelling work. Just keeping everything shipshape was relentless, and having boarders was like having house guests. You know the feeling when someone goes into your cupboards and helps themselves to a tea bag one too many times? You get mingy and bent out of shape about the small things. I worked hard all the time, mucking stalls, stacking hay, filling water buckets, putting horses out, bringing horses in, mixing grain and harrowing arenas, day after day in an endless cycle. On top of all the hard work, money was flying out the barn door. The hay alone set me back thousands of dollars. Then I needed a tractor and harrows, water heaters, hay feeders, buckets, poles, dressage boards and on and on. Every time I turned around I'd need to buy something else, and unless I had the barn filled to capacity, I wouldn't be anywhere close to breaking even. It made me a very respectful boarder in the years that followed.

My husband was a constant help with my Kingfisher venture and was very supportive. I think he enjoyed coming to lend a hand and being around all the activity—and without him it would sometimes have been impossible. For instance, in the summer we would have two thousand bales of hay delivered that we had to stack in the loft of the barn, and thanks to Murphy's law they always arrived on a day that was about thirty-two degrees Celsius. We would plug in the hay elevator that ran the bales from the ground to the loft. Then we would pull the bales through a small door into the loft, stack them and sweat. To add insult to injury, we had to wear long sleeves and long pants because otherwise the hay would scratch our arms and legs, leaving nasty welts. It was like doing a workout fully clothed in a dusty sauna, and it took hours. We would be heaving, lifting and pushing bales until our clothes were stuck to our bodies and our faces were a deep, dark red. But it had to be done, and the payoff was the exquisite joy of it being over. Taking a shower and being clean after that job felt better than visiting any expensive spa: we would sit and drink a cold beer on the back porch and feel like a million dollars. It was almost worth it.

I loved Ollie. There wasn't a day that went by when he didn't feel remarkable to me. But he was hard to be around, like an egg that wouldn't crack. He would stand in the cross ties and never look at me. He'd gaze straight ahead in a deliberate way. I wanted him to be my friend, but he always seemed to have one hoof out the stall door, ready to flee. I'd see other horses looking relatively happy but Ollie just looked consenting. Like a whale swimming up a river, he tried hard to be a dressage horse, but although his trot was extraordinary, his canter was not great, and there wasn't much I could do to make that better. His body was so tight and short-coupled that he was stiff, like an old man, and as we progressed it just got harder.

One day my husband's niece, Hannah, was up at the barn having a riding lesson with me. She loved coming to Kingfisher to help. That day we decided to free jump Ollie in the arena, just for fun. This is where you set up a line of a few jumps and let the horse jump them on his own. We led Ollie into the arena and let him go, which he thought was hilarious. He stood and looked at me, then turned and bounded off, bucking and rearing like a two-year-old. When he saw the jumps, he became focused and went at them like a hawk diving on a field mouse. They weren't that big, but he cleared them by about three feet, and our jaws dropped. His jump was a perfect bascule, and his body was completely connected in all the right places. It was spectacular. He jumped them so easily and looked so happy that I found myself standing there, cheering with Hannah, as he went round and round the ring, jumping them on his own. They say that horses tell you what they like doing, and that day Ollie showed us that he liked to jump; he had wings.

I had only been running Kingfisher for about eighteen months when my life took another great big turn. The first thing I noticed was that I was hungry and my jodhpurs were feeling tighter than usual. I was working so hard that I attributed it to getting stronger, but then I felt nauseous one morning, put two and two together, and the answer was: *pregnant*. While my husband and I weren't really trying to have a baby, we had an understanding that if it happened, we would let nature take its course. When I saw that positive test result, I sat and smiled.

Over the next six months, I decided to close down my boarding facility and bring my horses home. It was sad watching the boarders go, as we'd had some great fun, especially Carol and Erin, a mother and daughter who had become like part of my family. They were the kind of boarders who helped stack hay. That's a valuable thing. But all in all, the decision to close Kingfisher wasn't a hard one to make, since I was losing so much money. However, closing the barn was almost as much work as starting it up, and the whole thing took another toll on my marriage. My husband disappeared a bit more, and I wasn't sure if it was because he was annoyed about money or because of... well, I just didn't want to ask any questions. And those questions took a seat at the table where the other unasked questions sat, and they all got together and munched away at our joy. We moved around them in polite solitude and made plans. We were good at making plans.

Our farm was still fairly rustic and overgrown at this point, but we had fenced some paddocks and had a run-in shed. Although Ollie would probably have loved living outside the whole time, I wanted to bring him in at night because that's what dressage people did. We decided it was time to get more organized, and because my husband had bought a backhoe for his business, we got to work knocking down the old pigpens and clearing space to build a barn and sand ring. I didn't want a big barn, but I had no idea exactly what I did want until I saw a sweet open-plan building that Mennonites were producing down in Pennsylvania. It took some finagling to buy and get across the border, but eventually it arrived on a huge flatbed truck, like a large Lego set. The barn, a board-and-batten structure, looked very English. It had a tack room and three stalls, and it was open, so the horses could look out from under a big overhang. We added a bigger hay shed with a high roof at the end, and we put in some antique windows. I absolutely loved the set-up. I stained the barn a rustic brown so it fit in with the landscape. We had hanging baskets with flowers, planted trees in all the right spots and even made an area where I could give my horses a bath. It was perfect. I had my horses at home again and I was keeping them in style.

I kept riding Ollie while I was pregnant. It was fine until I got really large: I could get on, but I just couldn't get off. There was no way to lean forward to swing my leg over his back, so I sat there, beached. My husband had to come lift me off one day, and it was not very elegant. The riding was good, though, like a massage, and I trusted Ollie. It was as if he could tell that he had to take extra care of me.

My son, Angus Blue, was born in September 2007, and for a good year I slowed down and was just Mum. Our farm was the ideal place to look after a baby. We went for long walks every day along the dirt road, and that first winter I took him to Antigua to visit my dad.

My dad had been having an epic time on the sidelines of my life since I had moved to Canada, which was no surprise to anyone who knew him. He had ended up in Antigua because after ten years of bliss with the "intellectual" girlfriend, she had left him. He was heartbroken, which seemed to push him into a midlife crisis. He had loved the freedom of sailing ever since he was a boy, so he went to Russia and bought a tall ship. He then sailed the ship across the Atlantic with a hodgepodge crew and, after settling in Antigua for a few years, pronounced himself king of a neighbouring island called Redonda. His boat, the *Saint Peter*, was used in two of the *Pirates of the Caribbean* movies.

When I was in hospital having my son, Dad was so excited that he rang about twenty times. Visiting him was the one of the first things I wanted to do when Angus was big enough to travel. Being with my dad was like going home and reminded me of how caring he could be. He loved sitting with Angus on his knee and singing him songs. He was still young at heart and charismatic, but I also noticed he was slowing down. He was seventy-six by this time and still smoking twenty cigars a day.

When we got back to Canada, I settled into my quiet life. It was a relatively peaceful time, although it was sometimes overwhelming and lonely. My relationship with my husband took a back seat as we focused on this tiny human being, and I think we may have both heaved a sigh of relief about that. But having a baby at forty was exhausting—the sleep deprivation, as every parent knows, can be relentless. Walking to the back of our property and letting the horses in and out of the barn each day was my personal time. Grooming and mucking out the stalls became a peaceful activity, like yoga. It was my oasis.

As time went on, I started riding again, but I didn't feel much like training so I focused on Hannah and Ollie for a while. Hannah was only twelve by this point but a great rider. She had been training with me since she was seven and was full of determination and strength. She was formidable, and she wanted to jump Ollie. Part of me thought it was foolish to take her to a jumping show because he was way too big for her, but he was so well-schooled now that I thought, "Why not?" I trusted Ollie and knew that however excited he got, he would look after Hannah. It had been four years since he had done anything frightening, and we had mended a lot of fences. I understood him and could tell exactly what he was thinking.

The day of our first show came, and it was heartwarming seeing Hannah braiding his mane and washing his socks at my stable. It reminded me of my Barwell days. When we arrived at the show, Hannah looked quite pale, but she took the reins and jumped on board, her chin set. I felt a little sick as she went into the ring because Ollie looked beside himself with anticipation. She had no choice but to go full tilt around the course, and he just flew. It was magnificent. He was like a much bigger Stroller: he gobbled up the jumps in a flash of black-and-white thundering awesomeness.

Ollie jumping with Hannah.

When they came out of the ring, Hannah and Ollie both looked so alive, with big smiles on their faces; it was thrilling.

Over the next year we had a great time and took him to many shows, including some days out eventing where they won red ribbons. But one day we had an outing where Ollie stopped three times at the first fence, which was very unlike him. About a week later I noticed he was limping and called my vet. Ollie had to have some time off for a sore tendon, and Hannah drifted away and began playing rugby and wrestling, of all things.

When Ollie recovered, I continued my training in dressage, but it was getting harder as we got further up the levels. I hoped that when we got to Level 3 and could start using a double bridle, he might be easier to pull together. A double bridle has two bits and is a much harsher piece of equipment, designed to help the horse submit to the bridle. It's useful if you have a horse that does not give at that part of his body, and can make a strong horse feel lighter and more rideable. When the day came to try the double on Ollie, though, he simply wouldn't do it. I tried all kinds of different bit combinations, but I couldn't find one that he liked, and I was getting tired. I'd get off him every day with sore shoulders and abrasions on the insides of my knees because he was such a big horse to ride. It was like fighting a war—not with Ollie, but with compression. Like I was constantly pushing power into a smaller space, or trying to squeeze an orange into a ping pong ball. I was running out of steam. I also felt sorry for him. I knew he preferred jumping.

This was a busy time. I had a toddler who hardly ever napped. Then, out of the blue, my father arrived. He was sick. He had dropped a huge amount of weight and needed some help. I spent a whole year trying to get him a health care card. Meanwhile, his diabetes was taking over and his body was dying. Eventually he had to have his lower leg amputated. He took it all in stride, proclaiming that he would be like Captain Hook and get a peg leg, but about two months later his other leg began to hurt and change colour, and I saw him give up. We spent the last year of his life sitting in the garden at his nursing home, talking about life and dreams. My husband didn't come and spend any time with my dad and didn't show me much compassion, and I ignored it. I put it down to his being overworked because I didn't want to dig below any surfaces at that point. But it was sad.

Losing my dad was hard.

The day he passed away felt like a train was going over me slowly. After I got back from the hospital, I didn't know what to do with myself. So I took Ollie for a ride. It was all I could think to do.

The last year I had Ollie, I had his mind read. I know it sounds crazy, but there was a woman named Lauren Bode who went around the barns, talking to the horses. I have seen many skeptics become believers. When she met Ollie she said, "Oh my, you're a lovely guy." After a while she looked at me and said, "Ollie knows he's not very friendly with you, but he can't seem to bring himself to show you how he feels. He says he was beaten so much when he was a baby that he thought he was going to die many times, so he still feels scared all the time. But he wants to say thank you for looking after him." I swear that's what she said. Suddenly a flood of heat ran through my body, and I almost cried right there on the spot. But I couldn't because there were people around, so I pushed those feelings down and gave Ollie a huge hug. At that moment I thought I'd keep him forever.

Another year went by and my training had plateaued. I had the flying changes and could do most of the harder elements, but Ollie's canter didn't feel balanced or collected, so it was like I was faking being at Level 4. After much pulling and pushing and many tough rides and much deliberating, I decided to lease him out as an eventer. I wanted to see him happy, as I could tell he was also sick of doing circles. I asked around and leased him for six months to an eventer named Dawn, but that didn't last and then it was hard to find the right rider for him. So I used him to teach lessons on and to take friends out on hacks.

By this time I had bought another horse, Kandi Danza, who was getting most of my attention, and Ollie was spending way too much time sitting in the field. I had been dedicated to his every breath for five years, so watching him doing nothing was hard. He started getting fat and looking bored. I can't stand horses not doing a job—to me they start looking like they are being held captive, like polar bears at the zoo—and it was making me feel low. I decided that I was going to find him a new home as a field hunter or a jumper.

This was one of the few times that my husband spoke up. "We are not selling Ollie," he said one morning over coffee. I suppose Ollie had become our family horse. He was solid and comfortable in his life. I could put anyone on him and take him anywhere we wanted. He was also great with other horses on turnout, the gentle boss in the field, which was a useful quality. My husband had even taken some dressage lessons on him and had ridden him out on the odd hack. So Ollie was a member of the family, but I felt like the parent who has to walk the dog each day so everyone else can enjoy him. My husband and Hannah wanted to get on him once every two weeks or so and bomb around, and it was a lot of work for me to keep him fit in the meantime. It wasn't fair to Ollie. He was also fairly young, at only twelve years old, and I knew he could lead a whole other life with someone else if I found him the right home.

He wasn't mine; he was Ollie, and he had the right to feel useful and to have an interesting life.

My horse
I will get on your back
and know you tried
as hard as you could
You took it all
with a giant heart
your childhood
leaving you braced
You were massive
in motion
loyal
and I'm sorry
I let you go

Shortly after putting Ollie on the market, I got a call from a man with a strong Spanish accent, Sandro Cagnin. A few weeks later, on a dark, windy morning, a BMW sports car drove up my driveway. The most handsome man I had ever seen got out of it, looking like he was about to star in a Hollywood blockbuster. Part of me wanted him to buy Ollie right then and there because they would look so stunning together. Sandro had driven up to Ontario and was scouting around for a field hunter to join his club down in Hudson, New York. As he met Ollie and fed him some carrots, a raindrop landed on my cheek, like a tear rolling down toward my chin, but I brushed it off. We tacked up Ollie and Kandi and rode from my barn through the woods and out along the edge of the farmers' fields. By the time we reached the top field, the heavens had opened and it was pouring. As we turned for home, I looked back at Sandro to make sure he was okay. He was grinning from ear to ear, and Ollie looked like a massive Grand Prix horse going down centre line. They both looked so happy, alive and proud— and were sopping wet. I smiled and took a snapshot with my mind. By the time we rode back down my driveway, I knew Sandro was Ollie's new dad.

It was a big event in my life, selling Ollie, but again I didn't feel much. In fact, the only thing that worried me was that I wasn't feeling anything. For the first time I started to wonder if there was something wrong with me. But my ambition told me not to worry: it had bigger plans for me. My ambition knew that when Ollie was gone, I'd be able to buy another new horse that could join me on my dressage journey. I didn't want to admit that fact to myself because the guilt and shame would have been too dreadful. But when Ollie went, everything fell apart. He was the General and he kept some kind of quality control over my horse life. It was like I sold my left arm and didn't realize how much I needed it. But I paid for that decision. Dearly.

It looked like it was all going to be perfect for Ollie in his beautiful new home, galloping across the fields every day, jumping hedgerows in upstate New York, but the next few years were hard for Ollie and Sandro. I suppose I hadn't given myself any credit for how comfortable Ollie was with me, and he took a long time to settle in to his new life. He also found field hunting overwhelming and couldn't stand still, which is apparently a big no-no. I became good friends with Sandro, and I felt awful that Ollie wasn't what he had hoped for. Needless to say, he still loved him to pieces.

Ollie lives on a beautiful hill in Chatham, near Hudson, New York.

CHAPTER 8

Charles, 2005–2007

Sometimes I've wondered if I'm drama-prone—like accident-prone but more fun to talk about afterward. I have had some crazy things happen to me out of the blue, for no reason except that I was there at that particular moment. For example, one day I was driving home from the woods after taking my dog for a walk. It was an autumn day with deep grey skies and yellow leaves on the ground. I was driving north on a fairly major country road and noticed a stock trailer in front of me. Because I am a horsey person, I always take an interest in trailers: what make they are, how many horses they hold, what type of horse, for what discipline, and so on.

As I got closer, it was like I was watching in slow motion as the latch of the trailer door bounced up and the back gate opened. Then a horse came flying out, landing on the road right in front of me. I slammed on the brakes as the horse got up and took off toward the ditch at the side of the road. He made the decision to jump off the bank and landed right in the middle of a small tree. He pawed the air, then just sat there with a look of astonishment in his eyes.

I pulled over to the side of the road, jumped out and ran toward the horse in the tree as the man who had been driving the trailer came running back toward us. We stood there in silence for a few moments and then I said, "Should I call the fire brigade or the vet or…?"

Happy Charles.

He looked around. "Go ask at that farmhouse and see if they have a saw."

I didn't want to think about why he would want a saw, and I ran as fast as I could toward the farmhouse on the other side of the road. I knocked frantically on the door but no one was in, so I ran back to the horse. By that time the man was trying to work one of the horse's front legs back over a limb of the tree.

"If I can get one leg over, he'll struggle free," the man said in a strained voice.

And that's what happened. He pulled a leg back over the branch, and the horse thrashed around and was suddenly out of the tree. The man then led him up the road, the horse jumped back on the trailer, and the man gave me a friendly wave and drove off. That's when I finally closed my mouth.

Another time, I was driving west along Herald Road in the cold white dead of winter in my vw Golf. I noticed a pickup truck ahead of me with bags of shavings in the bed of the truck.

When you keep horses in at night, you need to bed them down. You can use straw or peat moss, but these days wood shavings seem the most popular form of bedding. You can buy shavings by the skid load, but when you run out you usually end up like the person in the pickup, hauling a load in your truck from the local feed store. The manufacturers pack them into plastic bags about the size of a bale of hay or a large suitcase. They weigh around thirty pounds. This pickup driver had been very naughty and had stacked them precariously high, with no sign of a rope or cable holding them down, and I think that's why he was driving under the speed limit.

As I caught up with him, everything again went into slow motion, and I watched as a bag of shavings shot straight up into the air, then hurtled toward me. It landed on the hood of my car and exploded in a blizzard of pinkish wood dust. It sounded like I had hit the sound barrier, and I ended up in the ditch, again with my mouth hanging open.

What were the chances? The odds of either of those two things happening at the exact moment I was approaching must have been a million to one. Was it luck or fate? I don't know.

But sometimes good things landed in my vicinity, and one of those good things was Charles. When I had Ollie, I decided to start buying and selling horses. My riding skills were getting better, and the horses were going well for me. I could teach a green horse most of the movements up to dressage Level 3, which means bending and lateral movements, extensions and flying changes. Online horse-shopping sites were addictive for me. They were full of horses of all shapes and sizes looking for new homes. There appeared to be many nice prospects for sale that were sitting in fields, not doing a job, and were maybe advertised badly. I'd look through the sometimes unflattering pictures and study the breeding, age and background of each horse. With some sprucing up, training and good photos, I believed I could resell a horse fairly quickly and make some decent money. Because I was still running Kingfisher at this time, keeping horses was relatively cheap; I could afford a sales horse, so I began scrolling through the online equine sales pages.

Since childhood I've had a thing for dapple-grey horses. I don't know why, but I love that colour, even though a dapple-grey horse gets lighter as it gets older and is extremely hard to keep clean. I also love iron-grey horses, the colour of steel. When I read an ad for a dark-grey Percheron for sale in Collingwood, I decided to go and take a look.

As I arrived, I noticed that the owner looked like she was about to have a nervous breakdown. She obviously didn't want to sell this horse. She led me around to the back of her house, through the snow to a large field, and called out a name to the horizon.

When he heard her voice, this massive horse came cantering from the far end of the field in big lolloping strides. He was so bouncy! She patted his neck and he just shone with happiness. I had never met a horse with that kind of energy before. His owner kept saying, "He's so special!" and as soon as I met him, I knew why. He was stunning, the colour of slate, with a high neck, short back and long, powerful legs.

She tacked him up in the field and rode him in a few circles, then handed me the reins. When I got on him, I was blown away. It was like riding a cat, with every limb working independently. It was an incredible feeling. He only knew how to walk and trot under saddle, but he did it perfectly: loose, supple and on the bit, like he was built that way.

His only drawback, as far as I could see, was that he was full Percheron, so he was very heavily built, and they had docked him, which means they had cut off his tail. People do this because back when these draft horses were used for farming, they didn't want the tails to get caught in the plow. Apparently this Percheron was meant to pull a cart or carriage in driving competitions at horse shows like the Royal Agricultural Winter Fair. He had been carefully bred so his temperament could handle the stress involved with working in a team of horses on the big showgrounds. But Charles, as I named him, was too small. He should have been about nineteen hands for that job, but he stood about sixteen hands, which was the only reason he was put on the market.

When I took him back to Kingfisher, my boarders looked at me with raised eyebrows. A few of them said, "Why did you buy that?" in a kind of small, judgmental way. I hate it when people use the word "it" or "that" to talk about an animal that's alive. I would look at them and say, "I bought him because he's the nicest horse I have ever ridden. Just ride him, you'll see what I mean." But no one took me up on the offer.

I'd get on him day after day and he would feel incredible. He was so clever and eager to please; it was all so simple. After a few days we were doing smooth transitions from one gait to another, and leg yields. After a few weeks I taught him to canter. This gait can be a problem for these big heavy types, so I had no idea what would happen, but it was delightful, light but with a perfect connection into the bridle, and in total balance. It was almost confounding. After four years of working my guts out on Ollie, I was feeling better on this great big grey horse after three weeks. And Charles was so fun and confident. He reminded me of the character in the movie *Elf*, sweet, curious and honest. He liked everyone and everything; he even liked playing with my dog! He made everyone light up around him.

The only crack I found in Charles's perfect demeanour was that he hated having his back feet touched. The previous owner warned me about this, and it was startling to see how he went from being confident to terrified in the flash of a hoof pick. He just didn't get it, or maybe he'd had a bad experience when he was younger. I could barely run my hands down his back legs without him darting forward and breaking the cross ties. When the time came for his feet to be trimmed by the farrier, he simply wouldn't stand for it.

A farrier, in my opinion, has one of the hardest jobs in the horse industry. They have to be almost as knowledgeable as a vet, and they must be meticulous; they need to have extraordinarily strong backs, wrists and hands, and they must deal with all sorts of horses, vets and horse owners in all kinds of environments. If a horse behaves badly, it can be extremely dangerous for the farrier who is bending over the hoof, because a scared horse can hurt a human in a millisecond, and farriers can't work if they're injured. Most of the farriers I've met have the patience of Buddhists around horses; if they get angry with a young or nervous horse, their job will be harder the next time they meet that horse. They can't lose their cool.

A horse needs a farrier every six weeks or so. Some horses go barefoot, which means their feet are just trimmed and rasped to keep them tidy and in good order. Other horses are shod, which means they have metal shoes nailed into their hooves. Some of the reasons for this are that their hooves wear down too fast or keep getting cracks, or the horse is jumping and needs more grip on the footing. Or they need shoes with studs if they are going cross-country, or...on and on it goes. In England most of our ponies were shod because we did a lot of riding on the roads. In Canada I seldom shod my horses unless they had problem hooves and really needed it. Sometimes I'd just do the front shoes, which helped the horse feel more comfortable, especially if the ground was hard. Shoeing can prevent bruising of the hoof. But whether they have shoes or not, they need their feet trimmed regularly. If you neglect this, the feet can develop problems and the horse may go lame.

Charles was massive, with big heavy feet. He probably weighed about 2,000 pounds, and Jamie, my farrier, probably weighed 180 pounds with his boots on. Needless to say, we had to work hard and fast to fix this problem, and we kept reminding ourselves that in every other situation Charles was sweet-tempered and lovable. I would run my hands down his legs for as long as I could, while a friend gave him treats. I'd make sure I did it every day, even if it was in the field for one minute. When the farrier was over to shoe or trim another horse, he would do the same, slowly running his hand down Charles's back legs and not trying to do much more for the first few visits. He would spend double his usual time and very quietly assure Charles that everything was okay. The next step was picking up his hooves and putting them down. That went on for another month or so. In the end it took four months, and lots of carrots, to get Charles's mind totally off his fear and flight response. One day I picked up his back hoof, and he curved his bendy neck all the way around and looked at me as if to say,

"Ohhhhh, I get it." And that was that. The problem was gone. Repetition was key.

After a few months I decided to take Charles to a local dressage show. I wanted to see what a judge would think of him. I saw a lot of whispering going on as I walked him into the warm-up ring. I think it was his tailless state that really got to people, but I held my head high because Charles was enjoying himself so much. He loved it all. I rode Training Level, and he did everything right. When I got my test score sheet, it wasn't a huge shock to discover that the judge could see what I was feeling, and I got the best score I'd ever had at that level. Charles won a red ribbon and looked very proud of himself.

Riding Charles was a delight, but one thing that became an issue was how much he sweated. After our rides he would be dripping. I decided it was probably because he put every ounce of his energy and love into everything he did, but it worried me. During the first winter I had him, he would be soaking wet and I'd be scared that he would catch a chill, so I bought a fancy blue cooler rug to put on after riding him. He looked at me like I was crazy, turned and tried to pull it off with his teeth. I swear he was laughing at me and saying, "I'm a full-blooded Percheron—put that away!" He was a big, tough warrior of a horse.

One of my favourite boarders at Kingfisher, who became a great friend, was Arlene. She was a tall, fiery blond with legs up to her eyeballs, and was a highly successful news anchor for television and radio. She was spicy with soft edges and had a great sense of humour. We had a hilarious time together, and she trailered with me to lessons each week with her Friesian cross named Liverpool. Friesians are the stunning horses that you sometimes see in Hollywood movies; they are almost always black, with a high arched neck, a huge, often wavy mane and fancy high-knee action. They are bred in the Netherlands and have a history as both riding horses and carriage horses. A Friesian can cut quite a swath in the dressage show ring.

Arlene and I could talk about our horses and the dressage world for hours. We had a saying when things got too serious in our training: "Last time I checked, I'm not going to the Olympics." But I think, deep down, Arlene maybe thought she was going. And part of me wondered whether, if the planets aligned, she might actually be good enough. She looked fantastic on a horse, and with her long legs, long arms and tiny waist, she had the air of an Olympian. Arlene had a whole other history, riding dressage ten years earlier and training with many of the top dressage trainers. She knew all the names and faces, but she had given it up after a run of bad luck and a loss of faith in the horse industry. She had bought this Friesian with the hope that she was going to waltz back into the dressage world, get to Grand Prix, have a Hollywood moment, and show 'em all. And when she got that Friesian going, he was very impressive; he could passage and piaffe, which basically means trotting on the spot, with the best of them, and it was spectacular.

Arlene loved draft horses, but even she would look at Charles and say things like, "You should buy a cart," which annoyed me somewhat. Nobody would give this horse a chance. It was like being given a suitcase full of money but having no one recognize it as legal tender. One day when I was in the ring with Arlene, I devised a plan. I said, "Oh darn, I forgot to give one of the horses his supplements. Can you just pop on Charles for a few minutes?" She was standing there with all her gear on. She shrugged and sighed, took the reins and jumped on. I came back ten minutes later and there she was, floating around. She looked at me in amazement and said, "I sold a Grand Prix horse for a lot of money to a dressage rider in the States. He was an amazing horse, but he never ever felt as good as this horse in the whole time I had him." I smiled.

I hadn't bought Charles to keep Charles. I had Ollie, and by this stage I had put possibly a thousand hours into making Ollie my dressage horse. Charles made me happy, and a large part of me wanted to keep him because he was so special. But horses are expensive, and I only wanted my one horse. Owning a second horse wasn't the deal I'd made with myself; my sales horse was to help pay for Ollie. Besides, in my mind I was more like a caregiver than an owner. I knew that I'd made Charles happy. He'd had a good experience with me and learned to be a lovely riding horse. I was truly confident that he would go on to make someone else happy too.

Of course, it wasn't going to be easy to find him the right person, someone who wasn't going to judge him by his appearance. I wrote a long ad and said it all. I knew the first person who rode him would buy him, and I was right. A sweet woman from Hamilton saw him and fell in love. She was honest and kind, and we kept in touch after he went to live with her. She saw the value in him that I did and recognized his beautiful aura. I was very sad to say goodbye to such a wonderful creature, but as I had always done, I just shook it off. I was enjoying the process of buying and selling horses. It was exciting and I wanted to keep going and buy another.

I didn't really know the value of my friendship with Charles or think about its importance at the time. I was busy moving on. But I still remember the feeling, the blanket of happiness that covered me and everything around us when I was close to him. It was wholesome, honest, unguarded and generous. I loved him, and I think he simply loved everyone. When I see him in my mind he is always wearing a top hat and tails and dancing with a big smile on his face. He had a happy soul.

Lucky Charles.

CHAPTER 8

You fell from heaven Charles
into my heart
I had to pinch myself
but I still didn't recognize you
at that moment.
I'm as bad as the rest
I should have held on to heaven

CHAPTER 9

Cooper, 2006–2007

When you own a horse, one of the most important things is to have a good vet. A horse, like a dog or a person, has to have regular medical upkeep, such as yearly shots against West Nile, flu and tetanus. They need their teeth checked and often rasped, which involves tranquilizing the horse and putting him in headgear that reminds me of *Silence of the Lambs*. Vets also watch for behavioural problems that may arise and check that your horse is being shod and fed properly. They often have to do heroic things like cutting a horse out of a fence line or delivering a foal that's breech.

Equestrian vets are some of my favourite people in the horse industry. To succeed in the job you need to have heart, determination and the mind of a detective, as horses can't tell you where it hurts. Vets also handle animals in pain, which can be extremely dangerous, so they have to be courageous, strong and thorough. I have never met a vet who isn't sparky to chat with—I think they need that to survive.

When I was growing up in England, we read books by and watched a television series about James Herriot, the vet in *All Creatures Great and Small* who had hilarious adventures in a small, made-up town called Darrowby. I'd watch every week, my eyes glued to the screen, waiting for a horse story to be featured on the show. The first vet I had in Canada was old Dr. Watt, and he

Cooper.

reminded me a lot of James Herriot. Dr. Watt was a tough old boot with a twinkle in his eye. Whenever he came to look at my horses, I felt like I was his favourite client in the whole wide world, but I'm sure everyone else felt like that too. He was enormously loved.

I remember he once made a call to Joyce's barn because a huge retired RCMP horse had fallen over and couldn't get up. This horse was massive and had been bought to do musical rides. He was coming in from the field, had slipped and was stuck in the barn aisle. He lay there looking sorry for himself, groaning and resting his nose on the floor. I was standing worriedly watching with a few other concerned horsey women, all of us wondering what to do. His owner was openly crying, thinking this was it for her dear old horse and that maybe he had had enough of this world. We put some warm rugs over him and stroked his neck and said nice things to him as we waited for the vet. When Dr. Watt arrived, he walked in and didn't say much. He got down on his knees, looked in the horse's mouth, pressed the horse's gums, peered into his eyes and put his hand on the horse's neck. He then stood up and asked us to remove the rugs and go get a shovel. Someone handed him one and he turned it around, walked to the back of the horse, swung the shovel like a cricket bat and walloped the horse's bum. Like a flash of lightning, the horse was standing. To this day, I have never seen a horse stand up so quickly. Dr. Watt handed the shovel back to the woman who had given it to him and walked out the barn door without saying a word. Maybe he was also a bit like Clint Eastwood, come to think of it.

When I got Chicky and moved into the dressage sphere, I fell into the care of Vicky Pringle, and she was my vet from then on. Vicky was one of the rocks in my horse world. She was beautiful in a Slavic way, and walked with determination, like she was going to get there first. Although she was tough and practical, she never came off as self-righteous, and she was kind. She also never shortchanged me or turned me down, and she had a great sense of humour. Over the years I had two horses show signs of colic, which, as I've said, can be deadly, and Vicky rolled up her sleeves and marched into the situation like there was an intruder in the house. She worked for hours, sometimes right through the night, making sure the horse was okay, and she didn't leave until she knew we were out of the woods. She would come out in the dark, in the middle of a snowstorm, to stitch up an injury, and she never complained. She was a hero in my eyes.

These days vets are equipped with all sorts of gadgets and devices to pinpoint problems, and their vehicles can be like hospitals on wheels. It's a huge industry and there are many big practices with tons to offer, but nothing can beat an experienced eye.

I always respected the vets who had seen many things. They were like walking encyclopedias, with incredible knowledge. They also had a lot of stories. Having a glass of wine with a vet is fun. I like to ask them things like "How many times on the job have you been afraid for your life?" and sit back to listen.

Buying and selling horses was proving to be addictive. I enjoyed every part of it, from finding the horse online to making an offer, schooling and training the horse, getting him fit and healthy, taking him to events and eventually advertising him and negotiating a sale. If everything went right, it was a great project. But we are talking about horses, so things sometimes backfired.

One of the ways I kept my costs down when I bought a horse was to not have a vet check, because that would cost another eight hundred dollars and eat into my profit margin. Not vetting the horse was a risk but, as with anything else, you shorten your odds the more you know. A knowledgeable horse person takes a close look at the horse they want to buy. You can tell a lot by observing the way horses are cared for and the way the owner handles them. You can stand back and take a good long look at their conformation and then take a closer look at each leg and hoof. But in my opinion, the best way to find out about a horse is to get on and ride. You can feel everything when you are in the saddle. You can feel if he is stiff in one direction or has a touch of lameness that the eye can't see. You can feel how fit he is, if he has a nice temperament and how much training he has done, all within seconds of getting on. I went to look at a lot of pretty horses that were ugly to ride and vice versa—you have to keep an open mind.

Many people would think that not vetting a horse is a stupid thing to do. In hindsight, they would mostly be right. But I was like a gambler and became so enamoured with the process of buying and selling that my life was incomplete without a deal going down.

The world of horse trading was so free and exciting. No licensing or law involved, just a handshake and some cash. Like the Wild West, a tiny bit outlaw, which was the way I liked it.

I had many really nice horses but also made some big mistakes and had some "crazy" horses come through my barn. I also found out again and again that people are sometimes barefaced liars. They will look you in the eye, shake your hand and rip you off. It was shocking.

Our next horse was Cooper, and even Vicky scratched her head with this one, although she had seen pretty much everything. As I've said, sometimes you have to be a detective—and sometimes it's a cold case.

My husband was taking more of an interest in riding at the time, and I thought Cooper might be a nice horse for him to work with as I was bringing him along to sell. When we went to try him, I made the mistake of not getting on. I thought it would be nice if my husband made the decision about his potential new horse, not me. That proved to be a mistake. Although who knows; maybe I wouldn't have noticed anything either.

Cooper was a tall Clydesdale-cross gelding who had been bought at the market by a blacksmith's wife. Clydesdales are a Scottish breed of draft horse that originated in the eighteenth century. They are hardy and strong, with excellent temperaments, so the breed spread through Britain quickly. They were popular workhorses and were shipped all over the world to be used as "draft power" for agriculture and road haulage. As with the other draft breeds, they almost died out as the world's agriculture became more mechanized, and by 1970 they were listed as at risk. Thanks to the many Clydesdale enthusiasts, the numbers have since increased. They are mostly bright bay with white socks and incredibly thick, furry fetlocks. To my eye they look more angular than other draft breeds, with long faces, square hind quarters and long forelocks. They are famous as the drum horses in the Life Guards of the British Household Cavalry, which is the King's official bodyguard, but most North Americans are familiar with them because of the Budweiser Super Bowl commercials.

Cooper was a bright chestnut with a flaxen mane and tail and a huge white blaze, very handsome in a Hollywood kind of way. He originally came from the Mennonites, where he had been used to pull a buggy. I didn't think about it at the time, but there is often a good reason why the Mennonites move a horse along. Sometimes it might be because said horse is not doing the required job, but if the Mennonites can't train a horse, that's a bad sign. They use horses for transportation, so they need them to be reliable and are good horse people.

Cooper was fairly cheap, because the woman selling him said she didn't want to keep him through the winter. I thought we had found ourselves a good deal. But I think when we went to look at him, we got bowled over by his beauty and didn't look closely enough. I also took the seller at her word. Her husband was my trainer's blacksmith, and I thought I could trust them.

When we got Cooper, it was winter and we were boarding our horses at a barn close by so we could ride in the indoor arena. Cooper settled in okay. He was underweight and green, which means he hadn't done much training. But he was so handsome, friendly and well-behaved that we all liked him.

My husband didn't work during the winters, so we would ride together in the afternoons. We were enjoying having a mutual interest again. But about two weeks after we got Cooper, one day, for no reason, he had a bucking fit. My husband leapt off, luckily managing to land on his feet, but Cooper kept on bucking for about two minutes, like we were suddenly at the Calgary Stampede. I called in Vicky and she checked him over. She found a small bump, like an ingrown hair, on his back. We removed it, he had no soreness and we carried on riding him.

A month later he did it again, bucking like a bronco with his head straight down, for no apparent reason. This time my husband didn't land so well, and he was sore the next day. I had Vicky look over Cooper again, checking his teeth and his balance. She gave him a close inspection and couldn't find anything wrong. So we checked his saddle, his bridle and his eyes. Nothing seemed to be amiss. We cut back the grain he was eating, just in case, but it didn't stop. Over the next few months, he would have sudden fits of bucking with no pattern or reason we could find. We discussed everything: strange diseases, brain conditions like Wobblers or epilepsy, or cold back, a condition where horses need to warm up before you get on them because they will buck when they feel weight in the saddle. But Cooper would sometimes start bucking at the end of a ride, so we couldn't figure it out. It was confounding. There is a point where I stop calling the vet in because it gets too expensive, and I try to figure things out myself, but this horse had us all stumped.

In the end we had him for nine months. We would get on and dangle our feet out of the stirrups in case he tried to press the eject button. I noticed over time a generally glazed look in his eyes and a lack of connection; he was just off. My husband gave up riding him because he couldn't risk an injury, and I think it upset him. He had wanted to be involved in my horse world again, like when we first met, but it had backfired and become another drama.

At that point I began riding Cooper to keep him going and noticed he was abnormally stiff in one direction. I tried schooling him—until he had a bucking explosion with me and I only just managed to get off in one piece. Then I asked my friend Andrea to ride him, but after he did it with her too, we gave up. We had spent a large amount of money on trying to sort him out, and I didn't want anyone to get hurt.

But now I had a different problem. I had to figure out what to do with him. I couldn't sell him, because he was dangerous. He was also too young to retire. It was such a waste. For a brief moment I thought maybe I could sell him to the rodeo. I ended up calling a friend who was a young horse trainer/cowgirl. I thought if anyone had the nerve and the skill to sort him out, it would be her. She came to look at him and he behaved perfectly. She smiled at me like she had just won the lottery.

There is a tradition in France that you can't give away a knife, because if that knife is used as a murder weapon, it could be argued that you still own the knife and are somewhat responsible. So I sold Cooper for a dollar, but at least I slept that night.

I told his new owner, "Just remember, it will happen when you least expect it."

A few years later I was parked at a horse show, and there was Cooper in the horse trailer next to mine. The girl who was grooming him said she had owned him for a year. I told her that I had once owned him and had problems with him bucking. She laughed and said, "Yes, he does that with me. I just hang on 'til he stops."

I watched her ride him that afternoon and he just looked all wrong. Like his brain wasn't connected properly.

I wondered if Cooper had been born that way or if something had happened. Maybe he had bucked with a buggy behind him when he was with the Mennonites. I can't imagine how that would have ended, but I'm sure it wasn't pretty. Horses don't forget, and just as happens with humans, a physical reaction can occur before they have had the chance to work it through mentally. Maybe when we were riding him he hit that stiff muscle and it made him try to remove the buggy that his body still thought he was attached to.

Sometimes a trauma is so deep it's unapproachable. One thing was clear: This horse wasn't able to have a conversation and tell us what was happening. Something big was taking over. It was bigger than him and bigger than us.

It was a shame and caused the Crow to start pecking away at some of its feathers in frustration.

I'd wanted to make my husband happy, but we were using horses as a distraction. We could talk about them and not us. We kept moving and building, and to some extent it worked. We were good together. After Cooper, my husband decided to renovate the house. He went at that project like he went at everything else, with absolute force and concentration. Soon I was living in a beautiful place. The tiny bungalow we had bought became an offshoot of a taller board-and-batten building with a steep roof and even a bell tower, like an old church. We transformed the space, and it was as if I had my Kerry Stables back. There was a big wall of windows looking out onto the backyard, and a bedroom with a balcony looking out into the paddock and woods. We had exposed beams and dark wood floors and a kitchen with bright-red counters. It was a house that I was very proud to walk into. I had a lot and I knew it. I was grateful. But I still felt that emptiness, that constant low hum.

Maximillian, 2007–2008

Another strange horse I bought was Max, a grey Swedish warm-blood crossed with Quarter Horse. I thought I would buy him for Hannah to ride for a summer, and then I would sell him.

He was boarded at a small farm near Beaverton, not too far from my place. When you try a horse, it's a good policy to see someone else in the saddle before you get on so you can look at the picture and make sure it's safe. In this case the owner's daughter was away at university, so they had no one to show him off. I was starting to be more careful about getting on horses I didn't know. Part of me could see a dark shadow circling above the saddle, waiting to feed off my bones after I made another bad choice. So taking Hannah was perfect, since she was strong and very determined, and she still bounced if she fell. She popped on Max and had a good ride, so I thought he would be a fun project for her.

When I went back a week later to pick him up, he made a great fuss about loading onto the trailer, and when he finally did get on, he had a complete panic attack. It's frightening to watch a horse lose its cool, but if they panic to the point that they lose their sense of self-preservation, as Max did, you know you're in trouble.

Trailering horses is, all in all, a frightening thing to do. Over the years I tried to figure out the safest way to load and unload horses, but in the end I came to the conclusion that there is no safe way

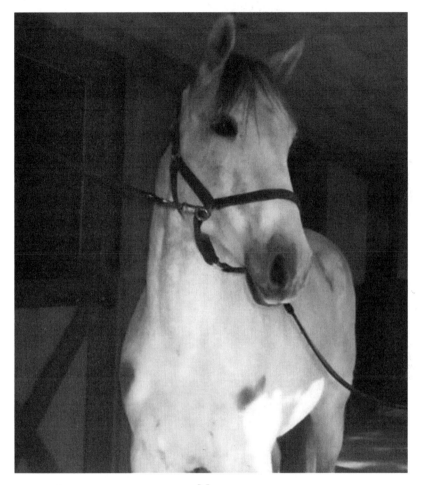

Max.

to get into a small, cramped space with a massive creature that can feel trapped. Some make this job easy, as they are happy to get on board, but many don't. Many aren't cooperative at all, and I have to admit I became more and more neurotic about trailering as the years went by.

Trailers are often designed for more than one equine passenger, and I think the designers of trailers presume that two people or more will be involved in the loading process. This isn't always the case. When you board at a facility, there seems to be a riders' oath to help each other load, but when you keep a horse at home, you usually have only one set of hands.

There are many kinds of trailers for every different depth of pocket. Some trailers are super swanky and even have living compartments so the rider or groom can camp on the showgrounds; some are bare-bones and just serve the function of getting from A to B. You can buy a trailer with or without a tack room or a hay rack on the roof. There are all sorts of inside layouts for different sizes and numbers of horses, riding side by side or head to tail. You can buy a small, lightweight trailer that can be pulled by a mid-sized suv (more popular in Europe) or the biggest North American beast of a trailer, pulled by the biggest North American beast of a pickup truck. There are hundreds of different options.

Part of trailering is training—accustoming horses to a trailer and leading them on and off, or feeding them in the trailer before you have to load them up and drive them somewhere—but if you are buying and selling horses, you don't know what you are going to get the first few times you load a new one. Getting into such close quarters with an unfamiliar horse puts you in a vulnerable position. But even when you know your horse, you can get into trouble; it's not a predictable thing to do. I would have sleepless nights before a journey, trying to figure out strategies for a good trailering experience, sometimes resorting to taking another horse on a trip as a buddy to keep the first one happy.

The first trailer I owned was a used bright-red, steel, step-up stock trailer. It had a big round nose and two compartments for the horses inside. I didn't know it at the time, but this would be the best trailer I ever owned. It worked for me because I could walk the horse into the trailer and turn him completely around, then tie his head up and close the gate, all without getting behind him. I had few problems with this trailer except that it was cold in the winter because the sides were open. But overall I loved it and took it everywhere.

After I'd had the stock trailer for six years and patched up numerous rust holes, I bought a two-horse straight-load trailer with a ramp. This trailer was a lesson in frustration because my horses would back off before I could do up the bar behind them. I talked to a few friends who said I had to teach my horses to walk in on their own and, I presumed, stand like angels while I put the ramp up. I tried grain and, well, it worked sometimes. But I didn't feel safe, and the thought of the horse backing out while I was trying to push the ramp up was more than I could bear. So I sold it and tried a slant-load trailer, which had similar problems. The horses didn't like being tied facing somewhat forward while I walked backward to close the slant gate beside them, and my horses backed up— sometimes reversing right off the trailer. I hated this because when they start to pull back it usually ends with them breaking the line that is confining them and they fight to get free. The best thing to do is let them back off and then try again. The process is complicated, but one thing is for sure: if you have been in a trailer with a panicking horse, you never want it to happen again.

When I bought Max, I still had the red stock trailer, and when I loaded him onto it, he reared up and hit his head so hard on the roof that he fell over. I got out through the escape door just in time as he flailed around, trying to get up. I should have taken him straight back off the trailer and said "no deal" to his previous owners, but I didn't want to look like I was weak. I had knocked the price down by almost half and we had gone through many negotiations, so turning around at that point would mean it had been a huge waste of time.

I drove home shaking with fear, thinking, "How am I going to get him off the trailer at the other end?" I knew there was no one at home at the farm to help me, and I didn't want to get back on the trailer with this horse. I could hear him kicking, like a thunderclap, any time we went round a corner or over a bump. I was sweating from the tension.

When I got back to the farm, I did the only thing I could think of to avoid putting myself in harm's way. I reversed up to the gate of my field and opened it, reached through the gaps in the sides of the trailer to untie Max's lead rope, then opened the outer door and inner gate to let him run out. That was the day I discovered that another advantage of having a stock trailer was that I could treat a horse like a cow at market. He took off out of that trailer like a missile and galloped around the field for a while, then came over to me. I gave him a carrot, put him in a stall and pretended that nothing had happened. But my heart was hammering in my chest for a good ten minutes.

Max settled in okay, but as Hannah worked with him, I couldn't help noticing that he was different. He always had a look on his face like he had just smelled something bad, and if I didn't know better I'd say he was looking down his nose at us, as though we were lucky to be in his presence. He did this in the field too; he'd stand away from the other horses like they were a nuisance and wait patiently to be brought in, almost like he was saying, "You go catch those stupid ones and then come get me." It was strange.

After a lot of schooling and getting to know him, Hannah and I decided to go out for a hack. We were just walking through the gate into my garden when Max got so overexcited that he suddenly squatted down on the ground and lay there with his back legs straight out behind him. I have never seen a horse do that before or since. Hannah jumped off and we waited to see how he would get up. For about five seconds he looked like a human getting up from a beach towel. It was a very peculiar sight. Once he was up, he shook himself off and looked down his nose at us, like he expected us to applaud—and maybe we should have. It was spectacular.

I also had a lunging incident with Max that gave me a few grey hairs. When I put him on the lunge line, he went forward, did a few circles, then stopped, turned, pinned his ears and came straight at me. Like I was his dinner. I stood my ground and swung the whip wildly at him. That brought him to a standstill, but he looked at me like he hated me. I've seen horses look at each other like that a couple of times, but to have him give me that look made me feel really insulted. I think I said, "How dare you!"

His behaviour was so peculiar that I phoned the previous owner and learned that his mother had died when he was a baby and he had been hand-reared. I did some research and found out that, yes, hand-reared foals often develop this exact temperament. He was confused about his identity and didn't think he was a horse.

After a few months we had figured out how to manage his quirky behaviour. It took a mixture of ignoring his issues and bending to make him feel happy. I tried for a short time to "win" when he did something strange, but I rethought that and decided that neither of us had to win; we just needed to get along. We took him to some shows and Hannah did fairly well with him, but we had to be diplomatic and put him on the trailer with another horse.

We sold Max after that first summer because even though he did okay, none of us ever enjoyed his company. The people who came to try him loved the look of him and sent their trainer to ride him the next week. She really enjoyed her ride on him, and I thought, "Well, okay then." He was the only horse I ever sold where I kept my mouth shut when they were trying him. I'm not proud to write it, but the buyers didn't ask me anything, so I didn't offer any information. I never heard from them, so I hope he worked out. When they came to get him he didn't want to load onto the trailer, and it took a lot of encouragement. But at least he didn't panic. He just objected. I'm not sure if we had made him any better in his time with us, but I was okay seeing that trailer leave my property.

Max raised a lot of questions in my mind about nature versus nurture because he was so un-horselike in many ways. But it made sense when I learned about his upbringing. To be raised by a human and then put in a field with equine creatures—how strange it must have been. He must have been so confused and at odds with everything around him. As time went on, I noticed that many people who met him felt that too. I suppose it was hard to be Max. I'm sure he tried to fit in at first, but maybe after a while he just accepted who he was. He put us in a place where he could handle us, and then he survived as best he could as an outsider. Definitely not human but not quite horse either.

CHAPTER 11

Silver, 2008–2010

A half halt is a quick setback or recoil a rider does to gather a horse in preparation for going forward. It's a movement you do all the time when you ride a show horse. You feel it in your hips, up through your back and in your outside elbow. Think of that moment of pushing a spring down to make the spring...spring. When a beginner learns to ride, a half halt might be obvious, as you can see the rider's movement and the change in the horse's speed. After a while, though, it becomes almost invisible. You and your horse need it. A slight pause for preparation and collection of energy. A moment of focus before moving past it. Most competition riders believe that a horse that doesn't listen to a half halt has not been trained properly, and a rider who doesn't use it has not learned one of the most important aids in riding. But sometimes you meet a horse that is so steady, with just the right amount of energy, that you forget half halts exist.

Silver was one of those. He was a good one.

His ad didn't even have a photo, but it read something like "Eight-year-old grey Percheron x gelding 16.1 hands. Can take him anywhere, sound. $2,000. Call Jack."

With my passion for the heavier horse type still intact, I called the number and had a chat with a friendly cowboy. He told me he had bought this horse from a livestock market in London, Ontario,

Silver on the day he arrived.

but he just didn't like him and wanted a faster horse. He said he had taken Silver on overnight camping trips on the Bruce Trail, a sometimes rugged hiking trail along the Niagara Escarpment in Ontario, and the horse did whatever he was asked, but he simply wasn't what the owner wanted. He also said that Silver had been a field hunter before, but apparently the previous owner had said he was crazy. My alarm bells were ringing quietly, but then he said, "I've had him for two years and he ain't done nothing wrong. He's a bit boring, to tell you the truth."

I thought, "Hmmm, when it comes to horses, I like boring."

I went to see Silver one cold December morning. It was a grey, slushy, windy day. When I arrived, the owner took me over to a round pen where a fluffy, muddy grey gelding stood with a big western saddle on his back. He was tied to the side of the ring with no other horse around, looking bored. This was an impressive start, as many horses can be what we call "herd bound." Herd bound comes in a lot of different combinations. Some don't like leaving the herd on their own and will keep calling for their friends. Some don't like being left behind, and some don't like either. Then you get the good ones who don't seem to care about any of that nonsense and just live their lives. A lot of horses would not tolerate being tied up in a round pen and expected to wait by themselves. That told me a lot about Silver already. He didn't even have any hay. He was just standing, waiting, like a good cowboy horse should.

When we walked into the pen, he looked around with his ears forward as if to say hello. I gave him a pat and took in his big soft brown eyes, good conformation and solid stature, and the clean, tight tendons on his legs. He was a nice prospect under all that fur and mud.

The owner got on, did a few circles, then jumped off and said, "He's all yours. I'll be back in a while." He pointed to a large field on the other side of the road. "You can take him in there if you want and take him for a run. He won't do nothin' wrong."

I thought, "Errr, right. I'll just stay in the round pen." I knew nothing about this animal; who knew what could happen. I got on, took a deep breath and walked him forward. The snow was blowing in my eyes, and I felt awkward sitting on that huge western saddle. But Silver was happy just walking around in the pen, slush sloshing about under his big hooves, his ears forward.

After a few circles I noticed I was enjoying myself, and I relaxed. Silver was totally at ease, which boosted my confidence. I pushed him into a trot and, after a few minutes, a canter, and that's when the bright golden sunlight came shining through the clouds. Actually, it didn't, but my smile did. I said, "Wow!" He had the lightest, purest, strongest canter of any horse I had ever ridden, like it wouldn't be a problem for him to canter on the spot. He was like another Charles but not as big and with maybe a bit more living under his belt.

I opened the round pen and took him out across the road and into the field. The snow was deep and the wind was howling, but he loved it all and so did I. He was bold and happy. I rode a couple of times around the field and went for a canter and then walked back to the round pen. What a great find. I made the owner an offer and took Silver home.

Silver settled in straight away and became good friends with Ollie. As spring swung in and the days grew longer, his fluff shed out and his beauty shone through. He was eye-catching, with big dark-grey dapples and a white mane and tail. Hannah fell in love with him as well and tried jumping him, but he didn't really like that job. This didn't matter to me because I knew how good he was going to be in the dressage ring. I concentrated on his flatwork, and he learned fast.

After about four months I took him to his first show, and he got off the trailer ready to take it on. A showground can intimidate a lot of horses because it's full of new situations. But he acted as if he had done everything before. I rode my test, and it was simple and easy. I got my first ever 9 out of 10 for one of the movements. Nothing was trouble.

I had a wonderful summer that year because Silver was dependable. I could invite a friend over to ride, and we would go out on the trails and I never had to worry. On a nice day I would even put him on the trailer on my own, go to the forest with my dog and hack for hours. It was such freedom to have a horse that was so easygoing. He really was a dream. Happy to go, happy to stand, happy to show, and he wasn't scared of anything.

As the summer ended and the horses' coats grew thicker, I knew Silver should probably move on to another home. But again, as happened with Charles, I was conflicted about selling such a treasure. At the time, I was training Ollie once a week with another high-level dressage trainer (Trainer 3). I'd been there about six months and we were still in the honeymoon phase and having fun. One day after a lesson, I was telling Trainer 3 about Silver. He looked interested and told me he had a client who was wanting to buy a horse. He asked if I would mind bringing Silver over so he could take a look.

For our next lesson I popped Silver on the trailer with Ollie and took them over. The trainer took a good look at Silver and didn't say a word. After a few minutes he turned to me and asked, "How's his canter?" I smiled and said, "Honestly, I think it's a 9." Trainer 3 didn't ask me to ride him first. Instead he jumped on and schooled him. When he jumped off, he had a big smile on his face and asked if he could keep Silver for a few days. He said he wanted to make sure he would be a good fit for his client. I agreed because I thought that by this time Trainer 3 and I were friends, and what could go wrong? Silver was so great that I knew he would behave perfectly.

But when I went back to pick Silver up, everything had changed. It seemed that after three days, Trainer 3 suddenly knew more about Silver than I did. Like he had discovered this gem. It was really annoying, like someone telling you they see something in your child that you've missed and, well, it was hard to stay breezy. I ended up having to transport Silver back and forth, time after time, and was never even invited to meet the prospective buyer. I was treated like a hostile seller, with no information of value to add, and I didn't like that at all.

They finally made me an offer and then asked me to bring Silver back again to get him vetted. I was open about the fact that I hadn't vetted Silver when I bought him, so they did a very extensive, expensive exam, with X-rays, ultrasounds and blood samples. Silver passed it all. Then Trainer 3 suggested I shouldn't be paid until the blood test results came back, in case I had drugged him! They asked to keep Silver at Trainer 3's barn for four days for the results to come through, then the following week sent me the board bill for those four days, and I liked that even less.

This was my first and only experience of selling through a dressage trainer, and the whole process gutted me. I knew why it was happening. Trainer 3 had to make it look good, like he was earning his commission from me. He was probably charging the buyer a commission too, so he had to take over the sale and make his client feel secure in the fact that he, Trainer 3, knew this horse. But it was like he was giving me a strong half halt and powering over me, the spurs ready to dig in my sides. I wasn't a professional in the dressage world. I was an amateur and was in the sport for different reasons, so I let him take control and said uncle. I allowed him to treat me badly. I should have been stronger and stood my ground, but I didn't want to fight. It was unnecessarily nasty horse dealing and extremely stressful for me, but I'm not sure Trainer 3 noticed. For him, this was the way things were done, and I guess he didn't realize the bond I had with Silver.

When I bought and sold horses, I never treated people like this.

I wanted a lot of money for Silver because he was worth it, but the most important thing for me was to make sure he went to a good home. I saw the emotional side of a sale and the fact that we were talking flesh and blood. I should have pulled out when they said I couldn't meet the buyer; after all, I didn't have to sell them my horse. But I told myself that the dressage community was small and I didn't want to upset anyone. Meanwhile, I was constantly upset during the process.

By the time the buyer made an offer and Trainer 3 took his commission, I didn't make as much as I could have if I had sold Silver on my own. It took a chunk out of my self-esteem, too, and I felt gouged and stupid. My husband hated the whole drama and couldn't stand the fact that this man was taking advantage of me. He called Trainer 3 and yelled at him at length about the concept of commission, honesty and losing clients. I watched him grow in front of me, and the veins stood out on his neck. He was so angry.

Silver at his first show.

More angry than I had ever seen him. He told Trainer 3 that he could shove his boarding fee—well, you know the rest—slammed down the phone and walked out of the house. We had been together twelve years and I had never heard him raise his voice. He was changing, and I just stood there and watched with my arms dangling down beside me.

I never took any more lessons with Trainer 3 and I never saw Silver again. I walked away and built the walls around my horse world higher. I missed Silver, though. He was so great. I had bought him eighteen months earlier from that cowboy, trained him and shown him. He had turned from being a trail horse to a dressage horse that made people's heads turn when we entered the ring. I had sold him for eight times as much as I paid for him but still thought I should have gotten more. I should have been proud of my success, but instead I wondered, "Why am I so useless?" I ran that thought in my mind on a constant loop. I could have insisted that I meet the new owners, that Silver be vetted at my barn, but instead I hung my head and waited for the experience to be over. I was, as usual, my own worst enemy, and I walked away deflated. I knew Silver would probably be fine and was sure the new owners would realize what a beautiful, special horse he was. But it was a needlessly bad ending to what had been a wonderful experience.

A few years later I saw Trainer 3 at a show. I wanted to walk the other way but I needed to know. I put my shoulders back and walked up to him and asked how Silver was doing. He said Silver was everything I'd promised and was loved and adored.

I smiled.

Beauty
under mud
you shone
and needed
all the love
that you
definitely
deserved.
I was lucky
to shine.
Silver.

James, 2009–2010

Dark horse
Dark shadow
Standing tall
And narrow.
You showed me
Pretty swift
Being cautious
Is a gift.
Being forgiving
Is a must.
Being giving
Takes some trust.

I loved buying and selling horses but didn't consider myself a dealer. It was a boutique business, which meant my horses were given a lot of attention. I got to know them and would sometimes give the buyer almost too much information. I wasn't in it to get rich. I wanted just enough money so I wouldn't feel like my training and showing were a burden on our bank account. Flipping a horse was a gamble, but buying one sight unseen was like shooting in the dark. You don't get to understand who the horse is from a video, and you can't feel the way he rides through a photo.

James after a spruce-up.

I knew all this, but I bought James from Ottawa sight unseen anyway because I couldn't find any nice sale prospects closer to home. My son was not even a toddler, and I still had Ollie and Silver on the farm, so going to Ottawa would have been complicated. I decided to take a chance.

James was a big, dark bay Percheron-cross gelding standing 16.3 hands. He was handsome and athletic. But here is a sweeping generalization: I think dark bay or black horses are trouble. At least they were trouble for me. My history with dark horses was, well, dark. Both Barnaby and Chicky had been dark, and I was getting superstitious.

I talked to James's owners at length before I bought him. They said he had been used predominantly as a husband horse, which is a term for a well-mannered mount that a non-riding husband can pop on if he wants to go out with his wife for a hack. It's a tiny bit sexist—but oh well. They also said that people often jumped on him bareback and rode him around their farm. The owner said he was really easy and sweet.

When James arrived, I was shocked. He looked dreadful, not at all like the photos of him that I had been shown. He was thin, with a dull coat, and he was filthy. I know that horses can go from looking good to looking bad in about three months if they aren't wormed or fed properly, so I didn't worry too much. He was bright-eyed, perky and good-natured. I checked his temperature, teeth and gums, and everything looked healthy enough, so I put him in the pasture with Ollie and Silver, and they all got along fine.

The next day the sun was shining, and I was excited to ride James. He was my new project and he looked like he was going to be a nice ride. I walked out to my barn and put him on the cross ties, groomed him and picked out his hooves. He stood still and was very sweet, nuzzling my hand as I gave him a mint. I tacked him up in Silver's saddle and bridle, which fit him perfectly, and he looked happy, ready to go. I didn't think twice about riding him, but when I did, I got on and fell off in about ten seconds flat.

What happened was I swung my leg over and asked him to walk on, but he got what we call "nappy" and pinned his ears back and walked backward. I had been told he was nice and quiet, so I didn't hesitate and kicked him forward. It was a reflex action but in hindsight a stupid thing to do. James jumped straight up off the ground and took off bucking, and I sailed into the air and landed on my tailbone.

When you're young and you fall off, it hurts, but when you are in your forties and fall off, it really hurts. When I hit the ground, I lay there for a while, looking up at the clouds, giving myself a hard time for the bad decision I'd just made. You can usually pin a fall on a moment's mistake or some bad judgment or other. In this case, I knew that riding James on my own with no one around was a dumb move, but I had thought he was going to be easy. Eventually I stood up. Well, that's a lie. I didn't stand straight up for about three weeks. I walked around like an eighty-year-old woman, and when my husband asked what was wrong, I told him I had tripped over our dog. It was one of the few lies I ever told him, but I was feeling foolish. Another blunder.

The next day I asked my vet to come. She said she thought James had stomach ulcers, so kicking him could have really hurt. "Hmmm," I thought, "maybe that's what happened—or maybe he's just evil." We put him on tummy meds, and I asked my friend Andrea to start riding him. She lived on my road and was a great rider. She would come in and help me exercise the horses, especially when I was nervous or injured.

Over the next few weeks, James worked well and Andrea thought he was a good boy. I tried to let the bucking incident go, but I didn't trust him after that. When a horse puts you on the ground, it's a commitment for them. I mean, he could have just bucked once. It's like a dog biting. They can bite to warn you or bite to cause damage. James had bucked to get me gone. I couldn't help wondering if this was something he had done before, and I didn't want to prove my theory right. The knocks and scrapes were adding up, and I was getting worn out. I hadn't had a fall like that for many years, so coming off James knocked more wind out of my sails.

About six months after I bought James, I put him back on the market. He was going well and looked great. As soon as the ad went online, I got a message from a woman wanting to bring her boyfriend to try him out. The showing went well, and a few days later the woman called and said that she wanted to buy James for her boyfriend's birthday but wanted it to be a surprise. She paid me up front and asked me to keep him for one month. I thought it was sweet and willingly joined in her plan; I had learned by then that sometimes you needed to nurse a sale. But keeping him after I had sold him was worrisome. I wanted to wrap him up in cotton wool to make sure he didn't sustain an injury.

Pretty much every rider or trainer I know has a story about the horses getting loose. It doesn't happen often, but when it does it's scary, and not just because the horses may be hurt. You worry about the damage they could do to others. For instance, if a car hits a horse, it can be devastating for the people in the vehicle. Farm owners spend a lot of money on safe and solid fencing, and horses generally don't seem inclined to jump out. They like to stay safe with each other in their herd. Because I mostly rode on my own, I had a perimeter fence, so if I lost a horse while leading him or if I fell off, he would be enclosed and not free to run onto the road. It was a precautionary measure and added some peace of mind.

About a week after I received the payment for James, I was in my son's room, getting him dressed. It was a sunny day and I was humming a tune when I heard a clip-clop sound coming past the house. I stood bolt upright, my alarm bells ringing. I ran to the window and saw Ollie's, Silver's and James's bums heading out of my driveway and down the road. I screamed, grabbed my son, ran downstairs and put him in his car seat in the truck. I then ran to the barn, found ropes, got a bucket of feed and ran back to the truck. I took off down the driveway. Then I looked around and tried to smile reassuringly at my little boy, who was sitting there with big eyes. He didn't utter a sound; he knew something bad was happening. "Everything's okay, sweetie, don't worry," I said as I sped out of the driveway in the direction I had seen the horses turning. I then phoned my cowboy friend, Justin, and asked for help. He said he would bring his trailer and be there as soon as he could.

By the time I turned onto the road, I couldn't see the horses anywhere, but as I drove along my road a neighbour mowing his lawn looked at me and pointed the way I was going. So I kept on driving down to Sandford Road, a fairly busy highway that many people zoom along to get to cottage country. I looked right, then left, and spotted the horses trotting together along the median strip, their heads up in the air and looking extremely happy, like they had finally found freedom. Ollie was in front, prancing along, his tail straight up in the air.

I turned and followed them, trying to decide what I was going to do. I had to make some fast decisions because I could see cars coming over the hill in the distance. I looked around at my son, a baby. Son. Horses. Cars. Death.

I did the only thing I could think of doing: I parked my truck right across the centre of the road, blocking oncoming traffic. Then I leapt out and waved my arms frantically at the cars to slow down. As they came to a stop, I asked one of the drivers to make sure my son was okay. I grabbed the bucket of feed from the truck and walked as fast as I could toward Ollie, shaking the bucket frantically.

By this point a few more vehicles had lined up and the horses were circling their cars, bucking and rearing, like they were showing off for the motorists. For a few long seconds they ignored me, but then Silver stopped following Ollie and turned his beautiful head around to look at me. He came to me like the lovely animal he was. I tried to act calm, but my hands were shaking so much I could barely clip his rope onto the halter. Then James decided that seemed like a good idea, and he also came over. But Ollie just circled, prancing around between the cars, missing them by centimetres. The drivers sat looking out of their windscreens with terror in their eyes, like they were watching a killer whale circling their rowboat. My heart stopped beating.

Finally Ollie stopped dead and looked away into the distance. I held my breath while he made his decision. He went very still, then blew all the air out of his nose in a loud snort and stood majestically proud, like the T. rex from *Jurassic Park*. For a split second I imagined his young feral self, running free on the prairies, a magnificent wild horse. Then he slowly turned his massive head to me, and I swear he said, "Bleah, boring," before coming over to me and the bucket of grain.

At last I had all three of them.

Despite this victory I was still standing on the edge of the highway, holding three horses, with my truck and baby in the middle of it. It was an epically nightmarish conundrum, and I was trying to pull answers out of thin air. Luckily, a couple of nice women got out of a minivan and offered to help. We came up with a plan for one of the women to drive my son home with her friend following in the minivan, and they'd wait for me there.

At that moment Justin arrived with the horse trailer. I handed him Ollie and Silver because his trailer could only take two, and I knew they would both be okay jumping on board. Off they went. The cars slowly pulled away, the people waving cheerfully as if everything was now fine. I smiled to the drivers and said, "Thank you for waiting."

But everything was not fine. I still had James, whom I didn't technically own or particularly trust, and I had to walk him home beside the highway. He was upset because the other two horses, his friends, had been taken away. Every time a car came zooming past, he would start jogging and jumping in the air, and I was worried I would lose my hold on his rope. So I walked him down into the deep ditch beside the road. It was tough going, with grass up over my thighs, and I had to be careful not to trip. To offset my anxiety, I kept my eyes focused forward, marched on and did something my dad always told me to do when I was in trouble: *sing*. Remarkably, as I sang, James began to relax, and so did I, but it was still the longest kilometre I have ever trudged. By the end of the walk I was quite fond of James. He seemed to understand the seriousness of the situation, and he looked after me.

When I got home I put him in his stall and thanked Justin. He gave me a hug, as I was obviously in a state. I looked around to see how they had managed to get out. I saw the perimeter gate wide open, and my old friend Klaus fixing the fence. Klaus was a local handyman who worked for me from time to time. He was an experienced horseman, but he was getting on and was starting to make mistakes. He had come over, opened the gate and just let them out. I looked at him and asked him to leave. I couldn't bring myself to be forgiving in that moment. I was livid.

I walked back to the house and my truck, profusely thanked the woman who had driven my son home, waved to her friend, grabbed my little boy, took him upstairs and finished getting him dressed. I took a quick look at my phone. Twenty-seven minutes had gone by. That was all.

After that episode I suffered my first real post-traumatic stress. When I heard any kind of rhythmical tapping sound, I'd run to the window with my heart hammering in my chest and make sure my horses weren't out. Even now, when I hear a similar sound I feel myself tense up.

James won some points with me that day. When his new owners came to collect him, I decided to have some fun. I braided his mane and put roses in it and left them a bottle of champagne at the barn. I loved how romantic the whole thing was. They were so in love with him and each other. It was sweet.

But it was a turning point for me because I began to obsess about the danger I was exposing myself and my family to. I had a great deal of guilt for putting my son in harm's way that day. Should I be doing this? The hits and misses were adding up, but the misses got the most airtime in my brain. I had made money with some of my sales, but I didn't like how nervous I was becoming.

My husband was also getting annoyed with the never-ending saga. He didn't understand my need to make money. Compared with what his company was making, my contributions were never of any consequence to him. He encouraged me to concentrate on my own goals and said he would look after the money end of things. But nothing comes for free. I slid into the comfortable space he offered because it was easier at that moment to allow him to take the reins, but with this came a touch more resentment for each other. We both allowed ourselves to shift into the darker parts of our nature. I got weaker and he got stronger. Any semblance of balance was dwindling, and we moved even further away from each other.

CHAPTER 13

Heiress and Beijing, 2010–2016

After Cooper went my husband stopped riding and concentrated on his business. He was doing well, getting large contracts and making huge sums of money, but at the same time he kept expanding his business. He got more crew and more machines and more vehicles, and the farm got busier, noisier, more dusty and less fun. Sometimes he would walk into the house with a big wad of cash and say, "Look at this," before putting it into a safe in the basement. He was spending money like I had never seen him do before. He bought a fancy wristwatch, kept his cash in a silver money clip and would always pick up the tab when we were out with friends for dinner. It didn't stop there. Every few days a new Thomas the Tank Engine model would appear as if by magic. Our attic was crammed with toys.

Part of me wondered if my husband was confusing himself with the super-rich clients he was putting in gardens for, and I worried about the money. I tried getting involved and asking questions, but he would clam up and tell me he had it all under control. One day I came home and there was a Volkswagen Touareg sitting in the driveway with a big bow on it. I suppose some women would have found that romantic, but I just felt sick when I saw it. It was like he was trying to prove himself with every move.—prove that he was alive , successful, and a *real* man.

My great friend Elizabeth Gillis about to go for a hack on Heiress.

When his landscaping season ended in December, he usually took two months off and we all went on holiday somewhere as a family. It was my favourite time of the year because we relaxed. But the winter of 2010 was different. I got involved with a local theatre company so I was less available, and I think he resented that I was having some fun. One morning he left the house at 6 a.m., came home around lunch and told me that he had been exercising polo ponies. I gulped. *Polo!* He had joined a small polo club near our farm and was "learning the ropes," as he put it.

At first I thought it was great that my husband was enjoying a new sport. The first week was only a few mornings, but the second week he went every morning and by the third week he was gone most days, all day. I was surprised by all this and tried to be supportive—until I met the Polo Guy who ran the club, and then I understood what was going on. My husband was being sucked into the same sort of addiction that I had experienced at the dressage barns, and he had a new best friend. The Polo Guy was charismatic and funny, but everyone around him was on tenterhooks because he could turn on you in a heartbeat. He was a man's man, and he was a time bomb.

Before I knew what was happening, my husband had bought a pony in the United States for a large sum of money and started acquiring the substantial amount of gear that you need for polo: saddle, bridle, breastplate, saddle pads, bandages, boots, rugs, lots of tape and many polo mallets. He also had to get the outfit, which consisted of white jeans and polo shirt, long brown leather boots, brown leather knee pads and a special helmet with a cage to stop the polo ball giving you a black eye. He was also socializing often with his new club members, going to fancy restaurants and events, and it was all a bit of a whirlwind. But, to his credit, he was really good at playing the sport. That first summer he was already playing in major tournaments. I would take our son to watch, and we would run up and down the field in between chukkers, treading in the divots. My son became good friends with Polo Guy's son, and I tried to make the most of it, but something wasn't sitting right with me. It was like the Crow had dived into my belly and kept moving and making me feel sick. This was not my tribe, and I looked at my husband and didn't recognize him anymore. By the winter of that first year he had two polo ponies, Heiress and Beijing, and he was playing twelve-goal polo down in Florida with the pros.

Polo is called the sport of kings because for centuries it has attracted royalty and the super-rich to its ranks. It is an aggressive game; riders often say it's like going to war, which isn't surprising since it's believed to have begun in the sixth century BCE as a training game for Persian cavalry units. Since then it has been played all over the world. Currently Argentina is the polo capital, with the best players and teams, and the UK and US are right behind.

A game usually involves two teams of four riders, and two goals set 300 yards apart. The game is broken into four to eight periods called chukkers, which last for seven-and-a-half minutes. There are four minutes between chukkers, and a nice break in the middle for champagne and schmoozing. It's a fast and furious event, and one reason it's so expensive is that each rider needs a minimum of three ponies to rotate through the chukkers. This is because the ponies are often going full tilt and it's hard on them physically.

Polo ponies are always called ponies, even though these days they are usually horses, over the height of 14.2 hands. They used to be smaller, and there were originally height restrictions, but now as long as your horse is fast and agile it can join the game. Most riders use mares because you need a pony that's a scrapper. They have to gallop around, chasing, pushing and bumping into other ponies while the rider swings around on their backs. Mares tend to look after themselves and don't get intimidated by other ponies, so they dominate the polo field. Polo ponies are incredible athletes and I have huge respect for them.

I had watched some polo before but didn't know a lot about it. It looked very dangerous to me, and I was surprised that my husband did so well, as he had always been cautious, even a little afraid, when we had ridden together. But Polo Guy had him pumped up, and he walked around with a definite bounce in his step. I would go to his events and offer to help, and he would shrug because he had hired a groom, like he was a millionaire. In all the years I had been riding I had never hired a groom and, well, I didn't like it. I wanted to be part of the action, not watching from a table with a white tablecloth, drinking champagne, wearing a nice dress and feeling weird. My husband paraded around after each game in his outfit, chatting and looking like a character from a Harlequin romance novel, and after a while I stayed at home and ate toast.

I knew that things would burn out. I'd watched it happen many times with money, horses and unrequited dreams. So I kept quiet until Heiress, one of his ponies, dropped a ton of weight. She was a beautiful 16-hand, four-year-old, dapple-grey Thoroughbred. Polo Guy had bought her from the racetrack after some good results racing. She had played polo for a few months and was sold to my husband. She was a stunning horse with lovely brown eyes, and very sweet. As the summer went on, though, she was not coping with being a polo pony and lost condition at such an alarming speed that her bum looked like a triangle, and you could see every rib along her sides. I couldn't bear it and nagged at my husband to ask for better care at the polo barn. He agreed. He was always kind to animals and didn't like seeing his horse look like she was starving, especially when he was handing over a lot of money each month for her board and training.

His relationship with Polo Guy was already turning a corner. He told me he was being used to subsidize Polo Guy's business and was getting worried about the amount of money flying out of his bank account, so I didn't have to wait long. Soon after he made that comment their relationship blew up, and he asked me to go over to the polo barn with the trailer to pick up the ponies and all his gear and tack. I didn't mind at all because I wanted my husband back and for everything to return to normal. Suddenly normal was looking pretty good to me.

As soon as I got Heiress and Beijing home, I called Vicky, my vet, and she came over to assess the situation. She wormed Heiress and we put her on a special diet with probiotics and lots of good hay. Within a month Heiress looked great, and after three months I had to cut back her feed. Beijing, on the other hand, was the hardiest little nutbar of a pony I had ever met and probably could have survived on air. She was tiny, standing about fourteen hands, with a cute turned-up nose and tons of energy seeping out of her veins. Because my husband wanted to carry on playing polo, I became his stable hand and exercise rider. I was happy to be helpful and relieved to see his horses looking well.

There are many jobs in the horse industry. I'd never been an exercise rider but I'd worked in many barns as a stable hand. Most of the time I worked the morning shift—feeding horses, turning them out in their paddocks and mucking stalls—which in my opinion is a wonderful way to start the day. Being a stable hand is a job that requires a lot of knowledge and skill but is usually paid minimum wage. It can be dangerous, as it involves machinery and is often dusty and physically demanding in outrageous heat and extreme cold. We were constantly battling the elements. But you end up meeting all kinds of people when schlepping it in barns, from wide-eyed pony-loving teenagers to salty old farm folk who need to make some extra cash. I met other musicians and actors trying to get by, but most of the time I met caring, hard-working animal lovers. Over the years I had many good friendships with very good people, people who only ever did things the right way and never took shortcuts or chances. I get why they like the job, because those moments when a warm breeze is coming over the fields, or when you finish mucking ten stalls and sweeping the barn, are satisfying, feel-good moments that I haven't experienced doing much else.

And then there are the horses. Most of them have a strong internal clock, so if they come in at 4 p.m., that's when you need to be there to meet them. If you are half an hour late, you might get into trouble because it's hard to catch a horse that's having a tantrum and racing around in a fury because dinner is late. Even worse if there's a few of them. There is a lot of responsibility when leading horses, because if you lose hold of one, all of a sudden there is mayhem. Some will race back to their stalls if they get loose, but others will take a tour of the grounds, and I've led many a horse to the field with it literally jumping up and down beside me like the ground is burning.

My job as exercise rider was to keep the polo ponies fit, as this is the easiest way to prevent them from injuring themselves on the field. Because polo players usually have at least three ponies, you often exercise them together. You can ride one and lead a few others at the same time—this is called ponying. Sometimes you see a groom riding one pony with about four other ponies on each side. It's like watching a stunt.

Exercising my husband's ponies was an eye-opener for me. They were a completely different ride from what I was used to, especially Beijing. She was like riding a sewing machine on speed, with no shoulders. It was difficult to estimate what her breeding was. She was dun (greyish brown) with a dorsal stripe and could have had some mustang in her, but all I know is that she was hilarious. In the year that I exercised her, I don't think she walked once. She was hot like Tabasco sauce but fun, and I liked her. Like Sonnet, she didn't scare me because even though she never stopped moving, she was brave and careful and I trusted her.

Heiress, on the other hand, was more nervous by nature and had a few issues. One of them was that she was very hard to tack up. Something must have happened to her when she raced, and putting the saddle on her was a two-person job at first. Every time I tacked her up I tried to reassure her, but she never stood still. She would start dancing, shaking and throwing her head around as if she were being bitten. It was ingrained in her being and she couldn't get past it. She also hated being left behind at the farm and would try to get out over her stable door if I drove my trailer away with another horse. It was sad, as she was easy as pie when you were riding her. In fact, she was almost too stoic under saddle, like she held in all of her emotion and went along with anything you asked of her.

About three times a week I would ride Heiress and pony Beijing, holding my reins in one hand and Beijing's rope in the other, and she would bounce along beside us. It worked fairly well, but after a month or so I invited my friend Alley to ride with me out in the top fields a few times a week. I did this because I thought the ponies weren't getting enough exercise going around my small paddock—and it was boring. I loved hacking with Alley. She was a good friend and also looked like a Swedish runway model, at about six feet tall and ten inches wide. She looked fantastic on tiny Beijing, like a cartoon character. We would set off mid-morning, listening to the crickets and cicadas singing in the long grass, and head up to the farmers' fields. Over the years I had created a secret path through the garden of our neighbour, who lived across the road. The path led through an overgrown dark wood and a boggy river, the mud sticky like treacle. Once we got to the other side and out of the woods, the sun would flood into our eyes as we entered the vast expanse of the fields, stretching out for as far as the eye could see. It was a magical place. We would ride along, chatting away, and arrive at the top fifty acres, then trot all the way round the edge and canter the whole field once before walking home.

Alley was a high-level rider and completely fearless. She carried me along on that wave, which was useful since it could have gone either way for me out in the open fields on these fiery beasts. They were like machines with an intent, and we never opened them up because we wanted them to think exercising meant nothing too crazy. We tried to keep them from getting too excited.

But one day we were cantering along side by side, and I said to Alley, "Jeepers, Heiress really wants to go." She replied, "Well, I guess that's what she was built for." I looked at Alley, and for some reason I smiled and put my hand, with the reins in it, a few inches forward. I knew that was the sign for Heiress to gallop, and off she went like a Spitfire.

Suddenly my eyes were watering and I couldn't hear anything, and memories of Barnaby came flooding into my mind. I looked back over my shoulder, and Alley and Beijing were leaping through the air like they were on a pogo stick. It took me a long time to pull Heiress up. I wrapped the reins around my one gloved hand and pulled with the other as I had done on Barnaby thirty years earlier. I straightened my legs and heaved. It wasn't pretty, but eventually she leaped and skidded and came to a halt.

I don't think Alley said much to me on the ride home. She was upset. But as we rode up my driveway I said, "I don't think I've galloped like that since I was a kid."

Her reply was, "I don't think that was a gallop. I think the term for what you did was 'going flat out.'"

Then we both started laughing, and she added, "Never do that again." And we laughed some more.

But that moment when my hand went forward was a sweet leap of abandon. A thrill that I hadn't felt for years. It sat at the back of my smile for a long while. I had survived and I was alive. For a moment I had let go—deliberately.

My husband continued playing polo for another year or so, but his love for the sport was dwindling and I didn't want to exercise his ponies if they weren't playing games. I began schooling Heiress because I thought she could be a good all-round riding horse, but Beijing was a one-trick pony and needed to get back into polo. It was hard finding her a home, though, because she was so spicy. She was more like a pro pony, and in polo, as in most sports, amateurs make up nine-tenths of the field, so everyone who tried her said she was too fiery. I thought she would sell immediately because she was experienced and good at the sport, but I was also a dressage rider trying to sell a polo pony. I rang polo clubs but no one wanted to take her on. It seemed their world was small and Polo Guy had a reputation, so as soon as I mentioned that was the club we played at, the door would quietly close. After what felt like a hundred phone calls that led nowhere, we ended up giving her to a friend who played. It was ridiculous because she was a top-class polo pony and would have been worth a small fortune down in the States. But in the end it was a good idea, as she has had a great life with the girl who took her.

We kept Heiress for another two years or so. She was easy to have around, like a dependable friend. We hacked her mostly, but sometimes my husband would dust off his polo stick and knock some balls around in the back paddock. I would watch her playing and think she didn't really like it, but she would never show it. Her behaviour was always simply consenting. I would have preferred it if she sometimes had a little buck or even put her ears back. But her past did not allow her to relax and show anything other than good behaviour. She was stuck in a permanent state of compliance. She never showed me her true nature or let me inside that protective wall. Not once. I didn't mind too much; it wasn't her fault. She stayed around and became a companion for the comings and goings at my barn, and I looked after her with an almost motherly protectiveness.

Long after I saw her for the last time, I read an article about Polo for Heart, a fundraising tournament in Toronto, announcing that Heiress had won the award for best pony on the field, which was a big deal in the Canadian polo scene. In the photo she looked fantastic, going flat out, chasing down another horse with a look of determination on her face. So maybe the polo life was okay for her that time around. I hope so.

Heiress changed my life in the end. In an indirect way she was responsible for the collapse of everything my family had built and dreamed about. It wasn't her fault; she was an unknowing pawn in a bigger game that, in a way, we all deserved to lose. But we will get to that later.

A good mare
fast like a hockey puck
with graceful lines
and forward ears.
You stood in my barn
a good girl
made by money
to be played by money.
An amazing creature.

CHAPTER 14

Simon, 2012–2013

I went to look at Simon because I wanted to find a horse to teach my friends on. I enjoyed teaching, and I thought maybe this would be a good way for me to make money, rather than buying and selling horses. Simon was a bright bay gelding standing sixteen hands. He had done a lot of eventing but was still young, at only seven years. He was an Appendix, which means Quarter Horse mixed with Thoroughbred. An Appendix is a lovely mix of these two great breeds, and Simon was a handsome example. He had the Thoroughbred eyes, long neck and longer legs, but the barrel and hind end of the compact Quarter Horse.

American Quarter Horses are known for their great temperament. Bred to run short distances, they were originally used to race. As the Thoroughbreds took over in the racing industry, the Quarter Horses were used as stock horses by cowboys because they are agile and great at cutting cattle. They are generally tough and sturdy and can turn on a dime. When you steer a Quarter Horse while riding in a western saddle, you often neck rein, holding the reins in one hand and moving them over the neck in the direction you want to go. They also have a gait called a lope, which is like a forward canter. They go with their necks long and low on very little contact, and they often have less suspension, which is easier on your back when you have to stay in the saddle for long periods of time.

The lovely Simon.

Simon looked perfect to fit the bill as a nice all-round school horse. When I drove over to see him, he went well for me, was well-schooled and nice to ride. Because he was young, I went back three times to try him out, just to make sure he was going to be good to teach on.

The day after I got him to my farm, I invited my great friend and riding student Elizabeth to come and meet him. It was a nasty day; a cold wind was blowing high in the trees and my husband's machines were running in the tree nursery at the back of the property, including a very loud tree crane and a large dump truck. I didn't think it would bother Simon because he had been so quiet when I tried him. I tacked him up and led him into the sand ring. He looked around a bit as I got on, but acted okay. After ten minutes I stopped and asked Elizabeth if she wanted to ride him.

I was excited for her to try him. She was an experienced and capable rider, but I could see that with her on board, Simon was getting tense. As they walked around the ring, one of my husband's vehicles made a loud banging sound. Simon spooked, then shot forward across the arena like he was going to jump out over the fence. Luckily Elizabeth stayed in the saddle and pulled him up, but I was shocked. I walked toward him, took hold of a rein and asked her to get off because he looked really frightened. I then got back on him, hoping that he might be okay because he knew me, but he felt like a different horse. His back was stiff, as if there were a steel rod running down the centre of it. Like he was going to take off again at any moment—so I took a good hold on the reins. After a few minutes I dismounted because I was beginning to feel frightened myself. I put him away and hoped he would be better the next day.

But when the next day came and I went to tack him up, his eyes looked like they were going to pop out of his head. We had a terrible ride, with Simon darting around and spooking at the slightest movement, and after that he didn't relax again for months. Riding him was like sitting on a toaster ready to pop. It was disappointing because I couldn't use him for lessons and now had another problem to solve.

After a few more rides I stopped getting on because I was feeling too jumpy and was sure I was making him worse. I asked Alley and my friend's daughter, Jamie, to ride him. They were both experienced eventers and both said he was okay but stressed. We couldn't figure out why his behaviour was so changed. Was it from that one bad day? That one bad ride? It didn't make any sense to me. I called his previous owners, but they said it must have been something I had done because he had always behaved well with them.

In an attempt to fix the situation, I stepped up his training. We took Simon to some clinics and events, but he was on edge about everything. He was frightened getting on and off the trailer and very tense on the showgrounds. Even hand-grazing was difficult because he would keep looking around, as though he were afraid something was about to jump on him. I thought perhaps he needed acclimating to different things, so I took him to even more off-property events, thinking the more he did, the less worried he would be. But it seemed to make him worse, and it wasn't fun being around him with his eyes too wide and his veins standing up. He was putting me on edge, and I found myself losing patience with him.

About six months went by, and one day when I was grocery shopping I ran into the girl who had shown him to me. She wasn't his owner but had been hired to school him over the years. She asked me how he was doing. When I told her he wasn't so happy, she looked upset and asked if I had a couple of minutes to chat with her. We walked outside to my truck and she told me that Simon had been a rescue case. He had been taken to market as a two-year-old with his brother, and they had been saved from the meat man at the Claremont Horse Auction. Both horses had been emaciated and close to death. When they got to their new home, they were extremely scared of humans and it took a long time before they even allowed anyone to touch them. Simon's brother hadn't been able to bounce back and had died, which apparently made Simon even more nervous. So the fact that he had become a decent riding horse was tantamount to a miracle. Before I bought him he hadn't lived anywhere but at the farm owned by the people who had saved him, so moving to a new home must have been very traumatic for him. I looked at her and sighed; everything began to make sense.

I had thought Simon was a tough Appendix eventer. Instead he was another Ollie. But unlike Ollie, Simon needed the pat on the neck and some reassurance. If I'd had that information, I would have treated him differently. When I asked why the former owners hadn't told me all this, she explained that they thought it might have put me off buying him, and they had really needed to sell him. I thanked her for letting me know and drove home.

Poor Simon. I went out to him in the field and spent a long time stroking his neck. I felt bad about the whole thing, so I decided to change Simon's story. I gave him two weeks off and only groomed him and gave him treats. We then took him out for walks with Ollie, no stress, and as I showed him more understanding, he became a happier horse. As I slowed down, he calmed down. After a while I began schooling him again, and he responded well. Before I knew it, I looked forward to riding him. He became my friend, and one day I discovered he was a hugger: he would stand with his head in my arms for minutes, his eyes closed, feeling my warmth. He was so sweet and lovable. He didn't want to compete or be a school horse. He didn't like change. He just wanted one mother and to feel safe.

I kept Simon for another year, but I was never completely confident putting any student riders on him. Eventually I sold him to a good home on the east coast where I knew they wouldn't push him too hard. I saw him a few years later and he was doing well; the new owners were very happy with him.

Simon made an impression on me, like a pattern left on my skin that is still there if I look hard enough. It seems I had been wearing the wrong lenses, and when I finally saw who he was, I discovered something I'd lost. I had forgotten that a horse could be a pet, a tamed animal kept for companionship or pleasure. To be loved. He didn't have to improve or be of value to be worthy of my attention. He was a horse, a living, breathing, thinking creature.

I was moving so fast, trying so hard to make my life seem valuable, that I'd devalued most of the things around me.

Simon was the Mirror Horse, but I didn't know it at the time; I was still trying to prove something.

I was still searching.

You were the Mirror Horse.
You set me up for understanding
That's what this was:
A reflection in the glass that I ran from.
Bolt
Walk away
Then stop,
Put your head in my arms.
Just hold me for a moment,
You said.

CHAPTER 15

Kandi Danza and Obi, 2009–2013

I'm moving back in time now to 2009. This was when dressage was becoming hard for Ollie, and I began looking around for a warmblood to train. I had noticed that there were more warmblood crosses being advertised on the internet, and I thought I might be able to afford to have one in my barn. But it was slim pickings, and I waited a while before finding a horse that had all the things I was looking for.

Kandi Danza was one of the few horses, like James, that I bought sight unseen. He was from North Bay, which was at least a four-hour drive from Uxbridge. The woman selling him practically begged me to buy him. She had dropped his price because she was going through a divorce and couldn't pay his bills. At the time, I was so bargain driven from buying and selling horses that it was like I was wearing blinkers. I didn't give her pain much thought; it wasn't my problem. I saw every purchase as an opportunity for me and didn't look past my excitement. I had become cold and unfeeling, without noticing the change in myself.

The woman told me she had bought Kandi from a breeder as a colt. He was her dream horse. In the video she sent me, Kandi's movement had a lot of natural suspension and looked very impressive, like he was floating above the ground. I believed I had found the perfect crossbreed. Although he was a bit small, he had all the qualities I needed to climb up the training ladder.

Kandi waiting to go into the ring.

When Kandi arrived, his owner looked exhausted; when she handed him over, I thought she was going to burst into tears. I felt awful about the whole thing for a moment. But I looked away and ignored it. It was as if I couldn't handle her emotion, and instead of saying something supportive I jumped out of the way and carried on like nothing had happened.

I was also transfixed by the fact that Kandi was possibly the ugliest horse I had ever seen. Nothing like the horse in the video. He looked like a turtle. His neck had no muscle, like it had been put on upside down, and he had a big belly, like he might have worms. I was taken aback. The owner explained that he had been leased out and they hadn't been taking as much care as they should have. "Oh well," I thought, "as long as he moves like he did in the video, the rest will come." I led him around the farm and the first thing I noticed was that he was pushy. He didn't respect my space, like he had attention deficit disorder. I put him in the cross ties, and he didn't stand still for a second. Overall, my first impression of him wasn't that great.

Kandi was a 15.3-hand, grey Trakehner–Thoroughbred cross with a tiny bit of Percheron. The Trakehner is a warmblood that originated in East Prussia (later part of Germany). They are known for being good competitors, but they can be highly strung. They were imported to Russia around 1925 and became a part of that country's cavalry. There is a saying that when Russian soldiers went to war, they arrived good and angry because they had to ride into battle on a Trakehner.

It took me a few days to work up the courage to get on Kandi because I thought that he might be terrible to ride. To my surprise, as soon as I was in the saddle he behaved perfectly. It was like he was relieved to hand his neurotic brain over to me and let me do what I wanted with it. I immediately liked riding him because he was fancy; after all the bigger-boned draft crosses I had ridden, he was easy and light, like sitting on a bouncy ball, and I fell in love.

Kandi was bred for dressage; his father, Kandidat, had been a successful dressage stallion. I had finally got my dressage warmblood, and it felt like I had somehow arrived. I was now able to join in the real sport of dressage because I had the right tool for the job.

When I turned Kandi out in the field, he put his ears back and went for Ollie. Ollie looked shocked and then turned into his stallion self for about ten seconds—teeth bared, ears pinned—and chased Kandi away several times. Kandi was completely overpowered, and Ollie was boss from then on. I'd never seen another horse be aggressive toward Ollie, so Kandi certainly had guts. But in everything except riding he was complicated. For instance, if I let Ollie out in the field before him, Kandi would go ballistic. If I took Ollie out of the field first, Kandi would go ballistic again. He would buck, leap and gallop along the fence line to the point of insanity, and I'd get anxious watching his antics, thinking he might run through the fence and hurt himself. It was frightening but at the same time tedious. Kandi had a lot of rules we had to follow.

At first it was worth it because I loved riding him so much. He had the basics down, which meant I could begin teaching him the fun stuff, like lateral work and extensions, and he was a fast learner. But Kandi was what they call explosive, which is also a Trakehner trademark. He was quiet and dependable about 99.5 per cent of the time, but if he had a reaction to something, it was huge. Because he was compact and athletic, he could move very quickly. I never trusted him as I had Silver or Charles. He was too unpredictable, like there was a little devil sitting between his ears.

About a year into our training, we were schooling one day when he stopped walking forward and instead walked sideways, like a crab, swinging his quarters in one direction. This had never happened before, and I immediately called Vicky, who suggested that maybe he was going through a growth spurt. At that point, Kandi was five years old, so a growth spurt was possible but unlikely. I gave him a month off and then started riding again, but a few months later he did it again. Vicky came out and did various flexion tests, and she concluded that he might have weak stifles. This was heartbreaking for me because I'd had big plans for Kandi, and weak stifles could put an end to them. The stifle joint is in the horse's back leg and functions kind of like the human knee, allowing the leg to flex and extend. Weak stifles can cause a horse to have a shortened stride or, as in Kandi's case, a reluctance to move forward. I thought maybe if I got him stronger, with lots of hacking and hill work, he would get better. But every time I pushed him too hard with transitions, he would need time off. Vicky came out and we X-rayed him, but it was all inconclusive. I had finally gotten my warmblood, but he was weak behind.

When he was sound, I took him to his first show. He was surprisingly good at getting on the trailer, but when we arrived on the showgrounds I thought he was going to keel over with excitement. I took my heart out of my mouth and got on him, and as soon as my bum landed in the saddle, he handed over his brain and was excellent. I could tell he wanted to prove something to a crowd. He was flamboyant, and he would go way better at a show than at home, throwing extra care and energy into his job. So I set a new rule: if Kandi was sound, I showed him. I took him to dressage events as much as I could, and we did well. He also looked better as his muscles got bigger, and I was really proud to ride him down centre line.

But being Kandi was hard. He had a look on his face like he didn't fit in, and he was always agitated. It was sometimes dangerous to be around him; he would do things like turn his head abruptly to look at something and clobber me because he seemed to forget I was there. He simply had no consideration for my safety. I thought maybe I was being too compliant with him on the ground and making this issue worse. Maybe he needed a stronger pair of hands to set him straight, someone who was better at understanding horses than I was. So I asked Justin, my cowboy friend, to come over and try to get Kandi to join up.

Joining up is a concept developed by trainers who have watched horses in the wild and figured out the pecking order in a herd. As horses are flight animals, it's used as a way to connect with their insecurity about being shoved out of the herd, which makes them vulnerable to attack. It has been described as the moment when a horse decides it's better to be with a person than to go away from them. I thought joining up might help Kandi pay attention to me when I was handling him and not be such a danger.

Justin was an excellent trainer, and I trusted him to help fix this problem. When he arrived, I explained what I was experiencing, and he nodded, took Kandi into the arena and let him loose. Kandi took off, galloping around and around and around, ignoring Justin completely. Justin tried to make him change direction and to move him away on the circle. But Kandi kept galloping, often running right through Justin's space, which was extremely rude. I could see

Justin's shoulders getting hunched, and he shook his head a few times. In the end he got Kandi's attention, and my horse slowed down and dropped his head, licking his lips in compliance, but it took a long time. As we walked back into the barn, Justin smiled and said, "Some horses are just difficult."

That wasn't what I wanted to hear.

Justin came back a few times, but progress was slow, and he admitted to me that Kandi was going to take a lot of work and it was going to cost some real money. So after a couple more tries, I abandoned the joining-up idea and became an expert at avoidance, figuring out how to keep Kandi placated and not get in his way. He was like a bad boyfriend; I wasn't going to change his behaviour, no matter how nice I was or how much good, hard work I put in. And like a bad boyfriend, in the end Kandi would break my heart.

One day, out of curiosity, I called the woman who had bred him. I asked if anything had happened in his formative years that could explain why he was so distracted. She burst out laughing when I said that and told me he was just a pain in the ass his entire childhood. All he did was bug the other horses and annoy everyone who handled him. So I surmised that Kandi was just Kandi and that was that.

As another year went by, I soldiered on and got him very strong and fit. It helped; we got up to Level 2 in dressage, and he was going well, light and forward. He was outstanding in some ways. For instance, horses can be impacted by the weather; when it's windy and the trees are blowing around, it's harder for them to spot danger, so they can become flighty and nervous. But Kandi didn't care about any of that. I could ride him in the tail end of a hurricane, and he didn't mind at all. I could also ride him past a field full of horses running and going wild, and Kandi wouldn't even look over. However, if a truck passed us on the road, he would jump into the ditch so fast I wouldn't know what hit us. It was all quirky, and I never knew what was going to explode his bomb.

I've had a three-strike rule with every horse I've owned because I don't want to die. A strike is an incident where I feel like my life is in danger. For instance, with Ollie, he had one strike with the bolt through the long grass. Silver had zero strikes. I was in my forties at this stage and did not want to get hurt again.

Here were Kandi's strikes.

Strike one happened when I was walking him from the field to the stable with Ollie. My dog barked near him, and then it felt like I was hit by a bus. Kandi ran me down, knocking me flying. I found myself on the ground under Ollie's stomach. Luckily Ollie just stood stock-still until I got up. Most horses don't run straight into you like that. They look after the people around them. If they didn't, there would be way more accidents. I was winded, bruised and angry.

Strike two occurred when I was hacking Kandi. He was a great hack most of the time, and twice a week I rode for miles up in the farmers' fields where we took the polo ponies. On this day, instead of trotting before I cantered, I decided to go from walk to canter for fun, and he exploded. He bucked over and over until I flew off and landed badly on my right hand, causing an injury that took almost two years to heal and is still not right to this day. Again, I was winded, bruised and angry.

The final strike happened when I was riding Kandi, this time in an indoor arena. Something frightened him—I have no idea what—and he took off sideways when we were walking on a loose rein. It was such a nasty thing for him to do. He did not take care of me at all. I could sit a spook or a bolt, but he did both at the same time with full force, out of the blue, and I hit the ground hard. This time I was winded, bruised and *really* angry.

But truth be told, Kandi's real strikeout was when he kicked Obi. That was the strike that finished our relationship.

After Ollie left for his new home, I thought that if I was going to continue training, I was going to really go for it. Because Kandi was intermittently lame, I decided to buy another horse. I also needed a second horse to keep Kandi company in the field. I searched the internet and found an extremely beautiful black warmblood called Onyx. Although I said earlier that black horses were not my thing, this opportunity was too good to be true. He was with a trainer friend of mine, who suggested to me that the novice owner had bought him on a whim and then discovered Onyx was too much for her to handle. He was affordable because he had sat in her field for a year and was not in great shape. My trainer friend said he was lovely and she thought I would do very well on him. I went to try him and couldn't believe my luck. He was stunning. Onyx was an Oldenburg, which is another German warmblood, 16.2 hands and twelve years old. The price tag should have been quadruple what it was, so I took the chance.

Like several horses before him, Onyx arrived not looking like he should, so I went to work fixing him up. I got him healthy and began my training. I renamed him Obi because my son was going through a Star Wars phase, and I thought the name suited him. There was something honourable and noble about him. He had a lovely long neck and a look of deep understanding in his eyes, like he was a master, the bridge between good and evil. I also had the feeling that maybe his life, like Heiress's, had been hard at times. But truth be told, I never had the time to understand who he was.

Over the next six months, I worked hard on my riding; by this point I was taking lessons promiscuously with multiple trainers. As far as I was concerned, I was training alone most of the time and wanted to keep my independence. I'd trailer to different stables and do clinics with different coaches but refused to belong to any one trainer. However, one coach I was hanging out with more and more was my good friend Dianne O'Brien.

Dianne was a Grand Prix–level rider, full of beans and standing all of about five-foot-two with her heels on. Her husband called her "the terrier" because she never backed down or gave up on any task. She had begun her riding career on Woodbine Racetrack, breezing Thoroughbreds, and was one of the few riders I met at that level who didn't have Daddy's credit card in her back pocket. She knew her horses, was tough and could really ride. She could get on the hugest, strongest warmblood and command its respect within seconds. I think they just liked her sparky energy and knew she was boss. I'd trailer my horses over to her farm in Mount Albert, and we had a great time working together. She loved Kandi, but when I took Obi over she got really excited. He was such a stunning creature.

Things were going well, all in all, except for one problem: when Ollie left the farm, Kandi thought he was now king of the hill, and Kandi was not a nice ruler. He was a bully on turnout, and often Obi would come in with a bite mark or two. This was concerning, and I did my best to manage the situation. Because I kept my horses at home, I could rotate the paddocks, which ensured that the horses always had fresh grass to eat. To mitigate any conflict between them, I turned them out for only a few hours in the morning, then rode them and put them back out in the evening. This way they didn't get bored or hungry, and Kandi left Obi alone. I thought they would get used to each other and it would all work out.

In order to keep training that winter, I moved them both to a nearby boarding facility with an indoor riding arena. It was my second winter boarding at this particular barn, so I knew the ropes. It was a small facility, with about twenty stalls, so the care was usually good, but it meant someone else was looking after my horses. During the first month that both Kandi and Obi were there, I noticed a few new shortcuts being taken, which concerned me. For instance, the owner told me she only needed one leg strap on the blankets because this saved time. I remember blinking and thinking, "Well that's just silly. Doing up two leg straps is not going to change the day's workload." She was also charging extra for little services, and when things start going down that mingy road, it often means the boss needs a new career.

After about a month, Kandi and Obi had a huge fight in the field. They had run out of hay, and Obi came in limping, with a big swelling on his leg. The girl working at the barn had seen what happened and said that Kandi attacked Obi. This was extremely worrying; if a horse kicks another horse, you always take it seriously. Horses know how to connect. A light or glancing kick is a warning.

When I got to the barn that day, I asked the owner if she could separate them and put them in different turnout paddocks, as I didn't want it to happen again. She shook her head and sighed, like I was asking for something I didn't deserve, and said it wasn't possible because she didn't have a free field. I asked if Obi could maybe go out with another group of horses because he was not aggressive, and she said, "I don't want to risk it." I asked again, and she said it was too difficult.

I don't know why she wouldn't change the arrangement, or why I didn't persist. It's basic stable management to move horses apart if they're not getting along. She had plenty of paddock space at her farm and plenty of options. I think it was because I was asking for more without offering to pay more. Maybe she was having financial issues, but in that moment I wasn't thinking about money. I was worried about Obi. It was an extremely awkward moment, and I said, "But I really think we should." There was uncomfortable silence. Like she was waiting for me to insist. But I didn't. And I will regret it forever.

Two days later, Kandi kicked Obi and broke his leg.

I was in Toronto when I got the call from the girl who worked at the barn. She was shouting and crying and it took a few sentences for me to figure out what had happened. I was shaking all over and drove as fast as I could all the way back and up to the barn, arriving just as Vicky was getting a large syringe from her car. She looked pale and devastated. I asked her if it was broken, and she looked at the ground and said, "Yes." Kandi had kicked Obi just above the knee and broken his leg clean in two. I knew with certainty that if there had been anything we could have done to save Obi, Vicky would have done it.

I walked into the barn and there he was, this beautiful big alive animal, shaking, holding his front leg up off the ground, and the terrible thing was that he looked pleased to see me. Like I could help. I cradled his head in my arms and said, "Sorry." Vicky told me to stand back as she gave him the injection. I looked away and heard him fall to the ground, and in less than a second he was gone.

I stood still and suddenly a lump came into my throat, and I started crying like a child. I was shattered. I literally didn't know which way to turn. I just stood looking into the stable wall, crying. Eventually I went home and didn't leave my house for a few weeks. I couldn't believe that I had let this happen to a horse under my watch. Kandi had given us warning signs, but they had been ignored. I was gutted.

That was the final strike.

I had no feeling for Kandi after that. I couldn't even hate him. I knew it wasn't his fault, but I shut down. He wasn't my horse anymore. I moved him to another barn because I couldn't face going back to the place where Obi had died. I also never wanted to see the woman who owned the stables again. She had taken no responsibility for what had happened. She hadn't even offered me my money back for Obi's board. Nothing. Not even a "sorry." She walked away.

My husband drove over the next day with a backhoe and buried Obi by the woods. It must have been an awful experience for him, and I finally understood how lucky I was to have this man in my life.

For a long while I couldn't see through my grief. The black wings of guilt and despair folded over me and wouldn't budge. I pushed and leaned against them, but they were closed around me. I sat in my house, waiting for them to open, trying to find a reason why it had happened. But during this time, my son kept me on schedule. He squeezed my hand without me asking, and one day, without realizing it, I squeezed back. My husband was also strong for me, and caring. He didn't rush me, and for the first time I leaned back into him and allowed myself to be looked after. We were a family and maybe that was enough.

Little horse
Loaded gun
Busy brain
Then none
Connecting
Burning bridges
Payment
For everything
I've ever done
Go away
Little horse
Run

I would love to write that I was a wonderful mother, but I'm not sure I had the tools at that point to be that nurturing, so the toddler years were hard. My son barely took a nap unless we were walking with the stroller or driving, so I was constantly tired. But as soon as he started to talk, I started to laugh and enjoy being a mum. He was one of those kids who kept close and was careful; he lectured me on good diet when he was four and talked like a twelve-year-old when he was five. We would have great philosophical discussions in the car. There was something about the car, and I was enamoured with his thought process from the get-go.

When he was very young, I introduced him to tennis. My family had been a tennis family, and I was hoping he would fall in love with the sport. In England I grew up watching McEnroe and Borg battle it out at Wimbledon, which was right up the road from the Kerry Stables. When the tennis was on, that's all you could hear at my house. My son took to tennis like I took to ponies, so we had a great shared interest right from the start. He began wearing a headband to hold the ridiculously thick blond waves of hair out of his face, and he had his proper tennis shoes, which he only wore on court. He dragged a tennis bag to practice that was almost bigger than he was, and he told me at the age of four that he was going to be a tennis pro. So tennis became a large part of my week, and I couldn't have been happier about that.

Although I wanted to take a break from horses, I had to figure out what to do with Kandi. The first time I went back to the barn, I could barely look at him. I walked up to his stall and, in his usual unsubtle way, he swung his head way too close to mine and I had to step to the side to avoid it hitting me. A blast of hate spread through me. Everything he did became insufferable. I had nothing good left in me for him.

I knew it was going to be hard selling a horse that I could hardly talk about. He was also, as I've said, intermittently lame, which meant finding a buyer was going to be a challenge. I thought it would be impossible to sell him to do more dressage, because at Level 3 he was going to have to "sit," which is a term for putting more weight on his hind end. Instead, I decided to see if he was any good at jumping and asked my friend Lisa to try popping him over a few fences. She hopped on him and after a short warm-up took him toward a cross rail, and he bounced over it like he had been doing it all his life. I asked Lisa to take him to a competition, because if Kandi could win some classes, it might make him easier to sell. The following week she took him to a hunter show. The judges didn't seem to like him. I think he had too much suspension for hunter; they like a less bouncy mover in that discipline. He went clear, which was good news, so we put him in the jumper class and he did well and brought home some ribbons.

I then advertised Kandi as an all-rounder at a low price. I think maybe the ad looked too good to be true, and the price was suspiciously low, so people could smell a rat. I was going to be open about his lameness but was hoping it would be something I could talk about in person when people took an interest. I finally found someone who wanted to buy him, but he failed the vetting—as I knew he would. What shocked me was how badly he failed and, in the meantime, he was sound.

I gave him the next winter off while I decided what to do, and I eventually leased him to an eventer. He loved eventing, and with his strong dressage training he often led the field, winning many competitions and qualifying for a big event in Kentucky called the Hagyard Midsouth Three-Day Event. He stayed sound for over a year. When the eventer decided to buy him, he failed the flexion tests and failed the vetting again. Vicky took more X-rays and ultrasounds, but it was difficult to see what was going on. We decided it was probably arthritis in his stifles, and although there is a lot you can do to keep a horse like this sound, no one wanted to risk buying him.

During that last year I rarely saw Kandi. When I did, it was to trailer him somewhere for an event, trial or vetting. I never looked him in the eye again. I'd circle him like he had an infectious disease. I wanted him gone so I didn't have to remember the horror of losing Obi. It had been over a year since the fatal kick and I was still raw, with a sprinkling of angry. I had had such high hopes riding Kandi, but I couldn't find it in myself to forgive him.

After a while, the eventing situation got on my nerves. Kandi was such a good competitor that the eventer's trainer took to eventing on him instead of the person who was actually leasing him. My horse was being pushed hard and doing well, but I wasn't being compensated. If I couldn't sell him and I wasn't making any money, why was this coach riding him at competitions? No one wanted to give me a penny to take on a horse that had issues, but they were happy eventing him every few weeks and winning. I had put hundreds of hours of training into Kandi and they were reaping the rewards. It was a good deal for them but not for me, and I knew that if he pulled up lame, he would end up back on my doorstep.

I wanted him to go away. No more Kandi! But he wasn't going anywhere. So I re-advertised him, dropped the price ridiculously low and told the people who came to see him that he had intermittent lameness problems and that's why the price didn't have another zero added. The girl who tried him loved him, and they took a chance. She was fourteen and a great little rider. I didn't tell her what he had done to Obi, but I did tell her that he could never go out with another horse. Over the next few years she sent me photos of her cantering through fields bareback on him and winning ribbons at shows. He went on to have a good life with her.

The day Kandi left for his new home, I watched him load onto the trailer and a blanket of humiliation dropped out of the sky and covered me. I had loved him, given him years of my life and my dreams for nothing. He had injured me deeply and didn't even have the decency to be worth money.

I watched them drive him away.

It seemed like too much. The frustration and sadness became a nasty taste in my mouth, like I was chewing on black feathers and wearing someone else's angry face.

Obi on the day he arrived.

I drove home and the next day picked up my guitar.
I thought that was it for me and horses.

CHAPTER 16

Fletcher, 2014–2017

I searched "Fletcher" on my computer, and this came up in a file where I write down my dreams:

I dreamt I went to see Fletcher.
I was going toward this long field.
The corn was high, making it like a tunnel.
I saw a flash of his face,
then he disappeared behind another horse.
As I got closer, I realized he had walked into a house.
I walked after him and went up the stairs.
But he was now a dog.
I walked over and started playing with him; he was so happy.
He rolled over onto his back and I scratched his tummy.
It made me feel so good.

When you ride dressage, as I mentioned before, you wear a specific outfit or "costume." Everyone wears the same type of jacket, which is like a tailored blazer. But when you reach Prix St. Georges (PSG), which is an international level of competition, you wear a jacket with tails, like Fred Astaire, also called a Shadbelly tailcoat. The coat originated in Britain in the seventeenth century. It's very posh, and wearing one had been one of my goals because it would

My friend Fletcher. *Aileen Barclay*

mean I'd achieved that high level of training. I'd worked my whole dressage life with the goal of putting one of those jackets on. When I began competing, people still wore top hats. It was a stylish look, but because of some severe head injuries the rules changed around 2013, and riders were required to wear crash helmets instead. The tailcoat remained, though, and I had never even put one on.

Six months after the Obi tragedy, I found myself back on the internet looking for another horse. I guess I wasn't done after all. My life didn't make any sense without a horse in it. We had everything sitting waiting for me. My little barn, my paddocks, my sand ring and of course my trailer. My husband had his polo ponies at the farm, so it was still in use; but it looked barren, like I had failed, and I didn't want to end the whole riding journey on such a low note.

By this time the pregnant mare urine industry was a shadow of its former self. The Pfizer drug company was feeling the squeeze. There had been some reports that hormone replacement therapy caused health problems, the price of shipping the product was increasing and the profit margins were getting slimmer. This had an indirect effect on the horse market in Ontario, particularly on the draft crosses that were so rideable and easy to keep. They had been part of the scenery and plentiful, but in 2014 I noticed there were fewer horses in general in the internet marketplace. The price of hay had been going up steadily, and beside the country roads the fields where horses used to graze were empty.

I wanted to find another Percheron cross like Ollie or Silver and spent hours searching all the sites, even looking at horses in Alberta and the United States, but nothing was coming up. Then one day I saw an ad for a Dutch warmblood gelding. There's a saying in the dressage world: "If it ain't Dutch, it ain't much." Dutch warmbloods are remarkably successful in the sport horse world. They have been refined through breeding programs that began in the 1960s and are some of the most successful dressage and show-jumping horses in postwar Europe. I normally would never have looked at a full warmblood because, in my experience, they needed to be pampered and, after Kandi, I wanted a low-maintenance horse. But this horse's ad intrigued me. It said that he was an eventer and had done well but had reached his potential. It went on about his exceptional movement and that the owner thought he would do well at dressage. He wasn't cheap, but the ad said his temperament was outstanding.

I was going to buy this horse using my inheritance from my dad. Kandi and Obi had emptied my bank account, and I noticed that my husband was getting into trouble financially. Polo had taken its toll, and climate change was also having a direct effect on his stock in the tree nursery. His business had grown so rapidly and had such large overheads that if he had a slow month, it could be extremely expensive. His company was tumbling out of control, but he kept the details from me. We had regressed to our usual pattern of behaviour: he kept quiet and I went to look at a horse. I looked over and past any problems we had because I didn't want to see them. I just moved forward.

It felt good getting in my car and taking off on a road trip on a crisp April afternoon. The sun was shining and the skies were a bright blue. I had to drive to London, Ontario, about two hours west of Toronto. When I arrived, I walked into a big old rambling barn and saw this handsome little horse standing in the cross ties in a warm wool blanket. He was a beautiful bright chestnut-coloured dream with unusual darker dapples, a white blaze down his nose, and big soft eyes. His name was Fletcher, and I liked him instantly; he looked like he was smiling.

Holly, the girl who was selling him, had raised him since he was two years old and cherished him, but she said he wasn't fast enough to go to a higher level in eventing. He also wasn't very big, maybe 15.2 hands with his shoes on. We tacked him up and went into a small indoor arena. Holly rode him for a while, and I watched and smiled. He was lovely. She was a nice rider but Fletcher looked a little lazy, and she added that this was the other problem: he was almost too laid-back. With absolutely no trepidation I put my foot in the stirrup and got on. His energy was all positive and, boy oh boy, could he ever move! If Kandi was like sitting on a bouncy ball, this horse was like sitting on four springs. When he cantered, I laughed out loud because he went straight up into the air and covered barely any ground at all. He was as fancy as they come, and if he had been a hand higher I would never have had the opportunity to buy him. Horses under sixteen hands are considered less impressive and are usually cheaper, but you don't get marked on being impressive in the ring. You get marked on being accurate. A smaller horse, in my opinion, is often easier to handle and, like a shorter person, can have fewer back and leg injuries. I'm also not very tall, so I didn't need a huge horse.

I got a good feeling from Holly and asked her every question I could think of before I bought Fletcher, to the point where she probably thought I was a little crazy—and maybe I was. You see, what I had discovered over the years is that people selling horses are like people going through customs: they don't offer any information. If you ask, "Has this horse ever done anything bad?" they will say no, because "anything bad" is subjective. If you ask, "Has the horse reared up on a rider?" they have to tell you the truth because you can go back and sue them if the horse is a problem horse and they didn't tell you. I remember asking, "So if I were going down a road on him, and an eighteen-wheeler drove past me at high speed, what would Fletcher do?" She looked at me and said, "Uh, I don't know." It was clearly a stupid question, but I was paranoid by this stage and didn't want another bad story. I really, *really* needed a good story. So I did something I had never done before: I asked for references and spoke with Holly's coach, her vet and the barn owner where Fletcher lived. I also looked up his show history and marks on the internet and studied many videos of him eventing. I did my homework. After all that, I had him vetted and then made her an offer, which she rejected. So I paid the full price. It all made me smile because I'd turned into the kind of buyer I found annoying. The buyer who's overly cautious, meticulous and pedantically sensible. I had changed and it worked because Fletcher never let me down.

When I picked him up a week later, I took my friend Elizabeth. It was a long day and very cold, but we were so excited, and everything went well. We got him home and put him in a stall, and he took it all in his stride. At first I was a little nervous riding him because he was very athletic, but as the weeks turned into months, my confidence with him grew, and I realized how lucky I was.

Fletcher loved hacking, and I figured out quickly that this was where he was going to do his best work. Some horses hate going in circles in the ring; they need stimulation. Fletcher liked outings and adventure. I made a routine where I would trailer him to a lesson with Dianne O'Brien once a week, then hack him in the farmers' fields two or three days, then school him in my paddock maybe once or twice a week. This regime worked; he got stronger and still enjoyed his job. He was a quick learner and exceptionally talented. We did some showing and he loved it. Everyone would watch us warm up because he was so beautiful—a bouncy, fancy, lovely, bright chestnut sight to see. At home he was sweet and playful. I put him out with Heiress and they loved each other, darting around playing halter tag, a game some horses play. I found myself always happy in his company.

But Fletcher was not totally perfect. Every month or so he would have a crazy day. He would wake up and be afraid of everything and completely on edge. I'd see the look in his eye and give him the day off, and by the next morning it was gone. It was almost as if he had to show me he was still a horse, that he could see danger one day a month. Usually, if he saw something that looked suspicious while we were out on a hack, he would prick his ears and go and investigate it—except on those crazy days when he would cower in the corner. I shrugged it off because—well, he was only human, after all. He was a brilliant horse; every time I tacked him up, I felt lucky. Like I must have done something good in my life.

That first summer with Fletcher was sunny and happy. My dream was coming back to me. I had the most beautiful barn, a great happy horse, a lovely house and the perfect family. After the many years of strain with my husband, I thought our relationship had become closer than it had ever been before. I decided the polo experience had made us both take stock, and we were going to make it—we had lived through a storm and would live to fight another one…together. That year it was his fortieth birthday, so as a surprise I got a babysitter and took him to one of our favourite hotels for a weekend getaway. I remember thinking, "I'm finally happy and so very lucky." The sun was shining on my life. I had it all.

Then winter came and everything exploded.

As usual, we boarded our horses away from home that winter. I was looking forward to riding because I had found Fletcher a place at a beautiful facility that had a massive indoor arena with really good footing. It was a little more expensive but it looked well worth it. We took Heiress to a smaller boarding barn close by that was cheaper. It was the first time I had split our horses up and boarded them separately. I only did this because my husband was barely riding at that point and I thought it would be a waste of money to take Heiress to the fancy dressage barn. But shortly after we took her to this boarding facility, he started riding a lot, which was a surprise. Then I remembered the cute younger blond woman who worked and lived at his new barn. I questioned him on his sudden riding commitment, and he responded emphatically that having new friends was good for him. And he began hiding his phone.

Just after Christmas, within one month of boarding his horse at her barn, he walked out the front door. I hung my head and knew I'd been a hard person to love, but I never in a million years thought he would leave and break up our family. Just like that. He didn't look back.

It completely side-swiped me.

Shame, guilt, sadness and unresolved feelings saturated my being. For the next two years, I was standing on the edge of a knife, and I experienced a slow decline into my first true depression, like a dark cave with no walls to lean against. I dropped twenty pounds and rolled into a tiny version of myself. But the one thing I kept doing every day, besides looking after my son, was riding Fletcher. My son and my horse kept me going.

Your long neck
smooth chestnut
with a mane of twenty colours
stretched out in front of me
ears pricked
over oceans of snow
on early grey afternoons
going and going
no doubt
your strength
your power
carry me
hold me up
take me away

Every year there is a huge southward migration of Canadian riders to compete in Florida. It's like the red carpet is rolled out and people congregate at massive events under the temperate, balmy southern skies and show their horses. That February I was invited to Wellington to do a lecture on freestyle music with Ashley Holzer, who at the time was the top dressage rider in Canada (she now rides for the United States). So I had to get my act together and go, because Ashley was, and is, a big deal in the horse world. It was exciting to book my flight and leave the frigid Ontario winter, knowing I was going to meet some of the top riders in North America and talk about music.

Wellington was like a movie set. I couldn't get my bearings, but maybe it was because I was wandering around with two heads, one swimming in this horse world I'd dived into, and one that had been kidnapped and was being tortured in the dungeon of my marriage ending. I was in a state. Luckily my trainer, Dianne, had taken her horse to Florida for the winter, and she kindly let me stay with her and gave me a shoulder to lean on.

The Palm Beach International Equestrian Center is the centre of the Wellington horse world. Set on sixty acres of grounds, it houses the show-jumping stadium and dressage arenas as well as polo fields, stables, restaurants, bars and pop-up stores. Surrounding these showgrounds are many equestrian facilities where coaches take their clients for a winter of training and showing. It's a scene where everyone kind of knows everyone else, and it reminded me of *Melrose Place*, but with more money. The humid, subtropical climate creates a very different landscape for keeping horses. There are insects that Canadian horses haven't met before, which can cause strange reactions or illness. I was also told that if a horse suffers any type of wound, the humidity means it can be hard to heal. But all in all, Wellington looked like horse paradise to me, with the open-plan stables, sand rings with white picket fencing, and palm trees swaying in the hot breeze.

On the first evening, I went with Dianne to watch the dressage freestyles, sipping gin and tonics in the owners' tent as the competition went on in the stadium below us. On the second night I was lucky enough to watch some show jumping with Trainer 2. The competition was under lights in a crowded stadium. We got to sit at tables right beside the ring, mesmerized by incredible feats of horse performance and skill. Everything looked glamorous, full of beautiful people laughing and having fun, all with very white teeth.

The Wellington horse calendar is big business. Prizes in a single season are worth nine million US dollars, some events bring in over ten thousand spectators, and throughout the season the park can see up to eight thousand horses. It's America, so it's huge! Being down there, as part of this colossal horse scene, was an incredible opportunity for my business, and I was hoping the milieu and the sunshine might take my mind off my troubles.

My lecture went well, and I enjoyed talking with the riders. Over the next two days, I tried to keep busy, but I was falling into a part of my brain that I hadn't visited before, and I couldn't seem to see out. After four days the dam broke and I burst into tears right in the middle of an important dressage event. I cried so much that I had to run out of the stadium and sit under a tree until it slowly subsided. I thought maybe, like in a movie, that was all I needed: a good cry. I got up, dusted myself off and walked back into the stadium with my chin up. But later that night I noticed it hadn't helped. I was just on my way down to the next floor.

On the fifth day I went home, alone, with a Florida hangover, to an empty farm that felt even colder than when I'd left. When I arrived, I stood in the kitchen and wondered what to do with myself. I didn't know what the point was anymore. There were pictures on the walls showing us all together, and I looked at them for a while. We looked so happy. I decided to take them down, one by one, and I put them in a pile by the door. The house suddenly creaked like old bones—the bones of the body it had once been. The next morning I lay in bed for a long while, then got up, got dressed and went to ride my horse. In the afternoon I picked up my son and we hugged for a long time. That's what I did.

I never brought Fletcher home to live after that winter. The farm became a place that didn't feel like mine anymore. I kept Fletcher at the fancy barn for a while and then moved him to Dianne's place, and we continued training. I took more time riding and grooming than I ever had before because all of a sudden I had hours to kill. My bond with Fletcher deepened. He was my rock, the thing I could count on.

Dianne was an immense help during this period. When you get up to Level 3 and beyond, dressage becomes tricky and incredibly intense. The higher levels require horses to sit on their hind ends, and it's like they are weightlifting every day. They start to gain mass and bulk up into superhorses. Every intricacy of their behaviour and daily workout is measured by the watchful eyes of rider and trainer, and you start to notice tiny things, like they go better on Wednesdays because on Tuesdays they get less turnout. Things can go right or wrong at any second, and you need your horse to be "through" to have a good day. I worked hard, and with Dianne's help we got Fletcher up to Level 4, the level before I could put on my tailcoat. He had the body and the brain, and I had the determination, but at Level 4 it becomes like a job.

As my life changed, an old problem that I hadn't faced for a while came roaring back: money, or lack of it. What used to be routine horse costs, like putting shoes on Fletcher or getting his flu shot, became fraught. Day after day, expenses were stacking up on one another, and I wasn't handling it well. I'd start to sweat and ruminate on small decisions for hours. Keeping a horse is expensive, and showing often adds three hundred dollars or more a day. I couldn't justify the expense, so I stopped taking Fletcher on any outings and just concentrated on training.

I was so close to PSG level. We had a fairly okay canter pirouette and a pretty good half-pass. We were also doing multiple flying changes, or tempi changes, at the canter—changing leads every four strides and three strides (four tempi and three tempi).

A flying change is a skip a horse does to change the canter lead they are on. It requires the horse to be well-balanced because they are shifting their weight from one side to the other as they change their lead. It's a hard thing to train some horses to do, especially if you're not completely straight as a rider. I always suffered from being tight to the right, so it took a long time to teach Fletcher that he needed to change his lead. He was comfortable cantering on the wrong lead (counter cantering), so he didn't feel the need to change leads, but the day he got it, he really got it and thought he should do flying changes all the time.

I was trying to string all the movements together. It was a little messy, but it was getting there. However, Fletcher didn't like the concentrated work. He missed all the adventures and hacks that we used to take. He started to suck back, which means he got lazy. But I pushed on for a good six months.

In the end, I guess I sabotaged myself. Maybe because I had stopped doing the things that, for me, made having a horse fun, I simply lost heart. Like Fletcher, I sucked back. I couldn't even find the motivation to do a circle some days, and I'd end up walking Fletcher around the field. He started to go not quite as well, and then not nearly as well, and then one day I was having a lesson, the sun was beating down, and I sank back to a walk and thought to myself, "I can't do this anymore." I got off and handed Dianne the reins and said, "Can you ride him please? I can't."

I was as close to a mental breakdown as I had ever been. My health was suffering from being on the "break-up diet," and my training didn't feel important anymore. My goals were insignificant compared with the new army of problems marching over the horizon toward me. Even though I loved Fletcher, I couldn't stand the thought of riding another circle, and the whole world of horses suddenly seemed like someone else's dream. Like I was a renter in my own house. I hadn't realized how rich I was until I wasn't, or how supported and secure I was until the rug was pulled away. I was floating around in constant vertigo. Lost.

Another blow came when my ex announced that I couldn't use our truck anymore, so I sold my horse trailer. Having my own trailer had meant independence with my horse, but I was past caring. Every time something like this happened, I would let it. I allowed my horse dream to be taken from me piece by piece, like dropping items of clothing to the floor one by one, as my new reality set in. I failed to acknowledge to anyone, including myself, that my life was important. My brain was sinking down to where I was worthless, like I deserved nothing. I was tiny, crushed and weak under one toe of the big black bird...

But Fletcher stood there in front of me each day, a striking example of success, showing me what I could achieve. Like he was shouting, "Look at me, look at what you've helped me become. I'm strong and ready." He was good, through and through.

Fletcher gave me the "ride of my life" twice. The first time was when I took him to a show and rode Level 4, the level before PSG. It was the last time I was ever in the show ring, and it was the ride I loved the most. I hadn't taken him anywhere for about six months, so he was really excited. About a week before the show he had come totally "through," raising his back in a way that he had never done before. He felt wonderful, like he was floating even higher off the ground. At the show we warmed up, and I was excited because he was so happy and forward. We entered the ring for the test, and he danced through the trot movements, doing everything I asked. When the canter tour began, I was close to heaven. But Fletcher thought in his happy state that it would be more fun if he did a lot of flying changes. By the time the test ended we had done way too many of them, including some tempi one changes down the last centre line. The judge stood up and applauded, and I burst out laughing as I took my final salute. You could tell Fletcher was just having too much fun. He had so much to give.

The second "ride of my life" was the day I took him for a hack and we just kept going, way farther into the woods than we normally went. We were exploring and his ears couldn't have been more forward. Then we came across this long path between some sumac trees. Like a tunnel. The footing was soft green grass, the sumac a deep dark red. I pushed him into a canter and we just bounced along, totally collected. Like we were running on the moon. As the path bent to the left or right, he would do an immaculate flying change. It was heavenly, like I had reached horse-riding nirvana. I suddenly understood what dressage training was for: not for winning a ribbon, but for this. This strength and joy that he had right then and there. He was a beautiful horse, out in the world, dancing to the rhythm of his own feet. That one ride filled about ten buckets of joy in my soul.

During those last months, I couldn't ignore Fletcher's value. I was looking down the barrel of a financial gun. Going each day to ride a horse worth a lot of money wasn't sitting well with me. I was getting scared that he might have an accident and be worth nothing at all, and then I'd hate myself because I'd have screwed up again. But I held on because he was my friend, and I tried to build a new dream: to keep Fletcher until he died of old age. I wanted to hack him and look after him until he got old, and then I would retire him and just go groom him each day and scratch his neck and love him. But Fletcher was young and had so much life ahead of him.

I circled around different scenarios in my head until one day I had an idea: I would lease him to another rider who could show him; then, after a few years I could have him back and find a place to board him by the forest and hack him until his back sank low and he only wanted to be given carrots. Out of the blue, a rider called Kelly came along who had the goal of going to the Pan American Games and needed a horse to take her there. Fletcher was that kind of horse. I was so excited for him, thinking he might go off and become a superstar. When the trailer arrived to pick him up, Fletcher looked so thrilled. He jumped on board with his ears pricked forward, and off he went. I watched as they pulled out of the driveway with mixed feelings; sadness for the end of my journey but, like a parent watching their child go to university, proud and happy for him.

Fletcher did well training at his new home, and I got good reports. Everything was working out as planned. It was a weight off my mind, which was helpful because I was going through a lot of changes. After over a year of staying at the farm, I decided it wasn't going to work. My ex still had the tree nursery there and was on the property every day. I hated seeing him. Worse, his new girlfriend would drive onto the property to bring him lunch. I made various angry threats, but the whole scenario was exhausting me. I didn't want to live my life like I was in a trashy reality TV show. Then one day I found out she was pregnant. I sank to my knees and gave in to the inevitable.

Because I didn't have a horse anymore, I decided the best thing was for me to leave. All our money was tied up in the farm, and because of his financial problems my ex didn't have the cash to buy me out. It's a complicated story, but we ended up buying another house in Uxbridge, a big old century home with a huge garden, at a very low price. Another bargain. I didn't need a house that large or want to take care of such a massive project, but I couldn't help myself. It was such a good deal. The only way we could make this work was to put both our names on each property. This arrangement would keep our heads above water and allow our assets to grow, but I made the decision out of desperation, without considering the full consequences of still being entwined with my ex, or of leaving the farm. It was another desperate, hasty decision and I threw myself into the move with all the fake deliberation I could muster. I wasn't myself. In fact, it was the furthest away from myself I had ever been.

I was so removed that I could barely see out, to the point where I couldn't even be there for my child. I found it impossible to hear him. I couldn't concentrate on anything. I tried to be a good mother but didn't have the tools, and my poor boy didn't get the support he needed. He was seven and thought his dad was a hero. He blamed me, was frustrated with me and missed his family. But he acted like he was stronger than I was and put one foot in front of the other and went forward. What else could he do? He still held my hand. In some ways, I think he found all the changes exciting and reacted to them one by one, not seeing the larger picture. He loved moving into town because we could walk to the cinema and the stores. He was able to make the most of it because he didn't have the Crow pecking at him. He seemed to have a large golden eagle sitting on his shoulder, and I marvelled at his outward strength.

After about six months of training, Kelly, Fletcher's new rider, had a tragic accident that ended her dream of riding at the Pan Ams. She was exercising another horse that spooked and bucked, leaving her with a bad neck injury. I was so upset for her, but when she asked if I could take Fletcher back the next month, my first reaction was shock. We had drawn up a contract, and I had taken out insurance for Fletcher—I had tried to take care of any potential problem that might arise if something happened to him, but I had never imagined that something might happen to Kelly. I didn't know what to do. I was barely scraping by financially and had just moved into my new house. Fletcher had now surpassed me in his training, and I wasn't sure I had the strength to keep him going. I hadn't sat on a horse for six months; it wasn't my life anymore.

When Kelly had her accident, Fletcher was down in Florida for winter training. I didn't want him to feel like he was being passed around, going back and forth between lessees, so I suggested to Kelly that she look for a prospective buyer. I knew that down south there would be a much bigger market in which to sell a horse like him. I told her if she could sell him for me, I would give her a commission. Then I waited.

This decision brought a lot of emotions to the surface. A large part of me still wanted to retire him, but I decided to change that dream on the fly because I was desperate. If Fletcher came home, I wouldn't be able to afford his board anymore, and I certainly couldn't afford training. I didn't have much choice. I put a large price tag on him—the kind of price that, if I got it, would at least be like a big pat on my back.

Of course, the perfect person walked in and loved him. I was happy and devastated. For the first time in my life, I wished that my horse would fail the vetting. I hoped there was some big problem, big enough that he would be worth nothing and I could have him back and find a way to hold on to him. But no. He passed the vetting and off he went into another life, and I couldn't even say goodbye.

It wasn't all bad, though. The money I got really helped. I bought a car and did some renovations. It also made me feel good in another way. I had bought a horse and sold him in the big leagues. Keeping him would have been the wrong thing both for him and for my family. So I put another Band-Aid on the place where it hurt inside and walked on.

After he was gone, I concentrated on my music career again, and I found a new love: writing. I folded up my breeches and put them, my jacket, boots and riding helmet into an old trunk in my basement. I sold most of my equipment and gave some away. But I kept a few things: Obi's halter and Fletcher's bit, my grooming kit, which had groomed all of my horses and still had Fletcher's hairs in the body brush, and my braiding bag with all the different colours of elastic bands and thread. I knew these small things betrayed the fact that I was hoping my horse life wasn't over.

It would be nice to say that I was happy and excited for my future, but that's not quite how it's gone. For the first few years, I tried to find a new relationship and thought that love would conquer all. But like my horse life, I wasn't able to make it work. For many different reasons, I would walk away each time.. One day I took a long hard look in the mirror and saw that I needed help. Too much was hidden and I didn't have any excuses left.

And that's when I wrote this book.

As for Fletcher, he is competing at Prix St. Georges Level in the United States with his new mum, Nancy Schmidt. He is loved and treasured, and is bringing home many ribbons. I think one day I will ask his new owners if I can go and say goodbye to Fletcher. I feel like I must.

It's a missing piece.

Maybe I'll wait until he's retired or maybe I should go soon. I don't want to ride him, I just want to stand and stroke his nose and say: Thank you for carrying me through.

Epilogue: The Why

My horse
My mirror,
Flight
Bolt
Stretch
And quiver.
All life
And courage
Wrapped up in fear.
The victim
The soldier
I see you
And wait
And smile,
Gather reins and
Ride away.

This book felt like it wrote itself (except for this ending, which I have now written eight different ways). It led me to places and memories that I had no intention of visiting, but I thoroughly enjoyed the journey. I'm sad to be at the end, as even writing about all these horses filled me with that feeling I know all horse-crazy people share. Like when I see a fallen log, I want to jump it; when I go by an empty field, I want to gallop across it; and when I see a horse, I want to run my hand down their neck. It seems like I'm surrounded by horses even when I'm not near them. They are a part of my soul.

As a horsey girl growing up and as a horsey adult, I'm not sure I ever got to the bottom of my feelings and asked some important questions. Like why? Why are some people horse mad? This book has given me the opportunity to do that.

A few years ago I was invited to a party at a dressage rider's house. We were gathered around, and some of the women were chatting about who was competing at what level, and so on. I was sitting next to one of those dressage rock stars, and she whispered to me, "Who cares! I'm so over it." I remember smiling, because during the conversation I had no idea who anyone was talking about. I was over "it" too.

I thought about that comment for a long time after that evening, and I wondered what the cost of "it" had been, my complete adoration of the sport and the relentless hours of training. "It" had brought out the good and bad aspects of my character. But for what? Where had "it" gone?

As I thought about "it," a clear answer came to me. The horses and "it" were two different things. Horses were a whole different form of life, and "it" was maybe nothing more than ambition. There's a strange feeling of shame when you think about losing something that had been so important to you. I felt like I had let "it" down. But maybe losing "it" would allow me to enjoy these beautiful creatures for who they are.

For years I have been carrying a bag of guilt about some of the horses I've cared for. I carried it for Barnaby, and for the tragic death of Obi. For selling my friend Ollie after I knew how hard it was for him to trust me, and for losing all feeling for Kandi. But now when I look at my horse life in its entirety, I see that I did my best. I trained many horses that were sitting in fields not doing any-thing. I gave them a job, and I truly believe that horses like work-ing, as long as the work is good work. I moved many horses on to great homes where they made others happy, so I'm trying to make peace with some of my bad choices.

It was important for me to look at the good stories as well as the sad ones: the fact that Fletcher is strutting his stuff on the dressage gold circuit, that Ollie is so loved, that Charles knew I thought he was the best, that Silver was cherished, that Simon was never put in harm's way again and even that Kandi brought a lot of joy to his new owner. All of it gives me a sense of fulfillment.

Each of the horses in this book told me who they were the first time I rode them. Through no fault of their own, or mine, we either jelled in some unfathomable way or we didn't. My problem was that I wasn't always a good listener. I was too busy thinking to lis-ten. I bought horses that I didn't particularly bond with because I thought I could make them into something else. Looking back on these stories, it's obvious that this is where I made some big mistakes. On many occasions I moved too fast and didn't want to see what was right in front of me. I lied to myself because I was constantly striving to be more.

Trainer 2 once said to me, "When you try a horse out, you should only bring him home if you are absolutely in love with him." If I had lived by that rule, I would have paved myself an easier path. But after writing this book I also have to acknowledge some of the great things that happened when I took a leap of faith. Sometimes it worked out, and I met many great, friendly, happy, big-hearted horses that filled me with happiness.

On weekends I teach kids to ride, and I find it interesting. Some of them are natural on a horse and some just don't understand, like their bodies don't speak horse. I never thought about this until I watched it over and over again. It has nothing to do with how much that child wants to learn; it seems to have more to do with compassion and feel. It's almost as if some people get on and don't realize that the pony is alive, while others get on and are immediately part of the pony. The same holds for the horses. Some are easy and open to learn; they are interested in what you put in front of them and are brave. Others can't seem to get the job done. They don't connect, and they don't know what you want— or they don't want to know. It seems they also have baggage from their upbringing, and sometimes they can't cope with what we are asking. It's a complex relationship with another brain that cannot speak human.

I've often thought that if I were a horse I'd be a spooky or jumpy one. I feel like fear has been nipping at my heels my whole life. But something occurred to me while remembering all these stories: maybe I was afraid of riding frightening horses because riding frightening horses is frightening. I wasn't frightened when I rode the horses that were brave. Brave horses gave me confidence and courage. Ride after ride, they made me feel stronger. Simple. Or is it?

When I was ten, we went to Devon for a family holiday. As we drove toward the cottage, I noticed there were ponies and horses all around, grazing in the green fields behind the hedgerows. We were going to be away for ten days, so I begged my mum to let me go riding. After a few days, when I did not let the topic drop, my mum popped in on our neighbours, who had two horses in their field, and asked if we could ride them. The neighbours were very friendly and invited us over any time we wanted. I was overjoyed, and the next day I talked my brother Ben into going with me to see the horses and take them out for a hack. One of the horses was bigger and younger than the other, so I rode that one. In my mind I had more "experience," even though I had only had a handful of lessons. I was ten; I had no idea. I was naïve and way too brave.

The memory is foggy up until this point, and then it becomes clear. We were riding along the narrow country road, heading into the summer sunshine, chatting happily as I reminded my brother to stay close behind me. I was wearing a sun top, jean shorts and plimsolls. We had to go down the road a ways before accessing a bridle path that would take us up into the hills. It was quiet. The odd car came along and had to navigate past us on the narrow Devonshire road, but we waved happily at the drivers and they smiled back. We were on an adventure, and it was thrilling.

Then a cloud came overhead, and in the distance I heard a different sort of engine hum, getting louder. My horse's ears went forward, and her head raised up a little, but we walked on until a big yellow tractor came around the bend toward us. My horse stopped and I felt her back go stiff. Then she spun around and took off. Suddenly I seemed to be looking out of my eyes from way back in my head, and I went still and started to slip. I found myself hanging off the side of the saddle, trying to hold on to her neck. She didn't like that and threw her head down, leaping and bucking. I tried my best to right myself, but I was too far over. Various scenarios shot through my ten-year-old mind, and I made the decision to fall. But because I was wearing the wrong kind of shoes, my foot got caught in the stirrup and I was dragged along the road.

Sometimes there is so much going on that you feel nothing but dread. I felt no pain and remember trying to claw at the gravel as if that might slow her down. When my foot finally came loose, I was smeared across the middle of the road. I lay there and looked around to see my brother's horse come belting toward me. I panicked and tried to roll out of the way just as his horse jumped to avoid me, but one of its hooves landed on my right calf. I clearly remember my poor brother's face, a mask of confusion and panic. When he finally stopped, he didn't know what to do, so he jumped off and ran to help me. I watched as both horses took off, galloping away and out of view down the road, their stirrups swinging against their sides.

I spent the rest of the holiday in and out of Emergency with bad road burns and a painful leg injury. If you have ever had a road burn, you know what an awful wound that is. The dressing needs to be changed every few days, and this was so painful that I had to be held down.

The interesting thing about this story is that I wrote this whole book and didn't remember it until the very end. It obviously didn't put me off riding, and I apparently didn't give it much importance. Or maybe I locked it away with all the other messy things that I find hard to deal with. But it could explain a lot. I was probably afraid of losing control from that moment on.

What brings tears to my eyes, and makes me think that this event was indeed important, is this question: why were a ten-year-old girl and her eleven-year-old brother out riding down the road on horses they didn't know? I was just a child. My beautiful, open, ten-year-old mind with its visions of joy, happiness and adventure was stolen from me by carelessness. Honestly, I feel angry just writing about it. I guess it was a different time, and we had a lot more freedom than kids get today, but where were my parents? When I put my foot in the stirrup that day, why didn't anybody say "Don't"? The balance between wanting me to be independent and making sure I didn't get hurt was missing. I was encouraged to make choices based purely on living life to its fullest, not on looking after myself. I realize now that I should have been more careful when making large decisions, but like others in my family I'm good at throwing caution to the wind. Odds are that when you do that, some of the time the wind will come back and blow you over.

This book wasn't meant to be some kind of strange self-help thing; it was meant to be about the horses. Actually, when I started writing, it was going to be about the horse industry. But if you're a writer, you know that the inner workings of your mind tend to push through your words because they want to be heard. I suppose what I've learned from all this is that details, upbringing and choices are important. I could have made better decisions, but I didn't because I was injured. I have been stuck in a pattern, swinging off that horse's neck and trying to get back on board.

We are a mirror of our experiences. Each horse was a mirror to parts of my life and my actions, and each one showed me how to deal with a different scenario. But it was when I wrote about Simon that it became obvious I needed some compassion. I'm not all right without it. I'm not tough. I'm not independent. I'm still just a kid in the scheme of things. Simon's was the first story that made me think about the mirror. He made me start wondering about these stories and what they really mean.

There was a distance in my family that we all felt. It was passed down from a time when children were seen and not heard, and I think it exists for a lot of people today. Maybe that's why I wanted to care for these creatures, because being close to humans has been hard for me. But it's funny, because being close to horses is also hard. They aren't like dogs or cats; they are more abstract. Maybe I was comfortable loving something that was aloof. Or maybe I was unable to deeply connect.

It's time for me to hold the reins, break some patterns, feel compassion and love.

I tried to be a good mother to my horses, and I'm trying to be a better mother to myself, and to my son. It's an ongoing attempt, and who knows how it will turn out. People like me work hard to find things to fill our hearts, and then walk away because we feel undeserving. I think I need to give myself that hug I gave Simon, or maybe, like Ollie, I need a wallop. Maybe this book is my hug, or maybe it's both.

Hacking with Fletcher.

Someone said to me recently that I was born with a silver spoon in my mouth. The comment stopped me in my tracks. I know I was lucky to have had all these horses in my life, and I know many people have never had the opportunity to even sit on a horse. But I don't think this book is really about the horses. This could be about any ambitious pursuit. Any interest that you obsess over. Any narrowing of vision that allows you to not look too deeply into what's really hurting you.

My horse world stopped when it did, but it might not have. Another me could still be untacking Fletcher and going to have dinner with a man who gives me just enough to keep me from digging too deep. Having another glass of wine and talking about my daily ride. Living under the shadow of that big dark wing. Hiding.

There was a comfort there, but maybe being comfortable in life is not the point. Maybe connection is the point, and you can't connect if you have removed yourself from the conversation.

Anyway. I could go on...

So, why horses? Why this fascination? What makes us horse crazy?

My answer is: Maybe it's that need for connection. Maybe the need to feel important. To be a mother. To show love. To have control. Maybe it's to do with adrenaline and adventure. To feel alive. Maybe it's the freedom, or the feeling that you have stepped back in time. Maybe it's the smells, the fresh air and the tightening of a girth. The shine on their coats after you've groomed them. The sound they make when they canter up a steep hill, or when they chew their grain. The feeling you get when you stand beside a gentle giant. Maybe it's none of those things.

But one thing I can tell you for sure is that it's just like falling in love. And I've been lucky enough to have fallen in love many times.

I never
Till now
Understood
That I rode
From feelings

EPILOGUE: THE WHY

On a galloping horse
That has kept running
Until the last page was turned.

The End

Disclaimer

This is an opinionated memoir. The views and perspectives are mine alone. I would love to receive feedback from you if you have a different view, but voiced in a way that understands that I do admit to many occasions where I could have acted in a better way toward these beautiful creatures. If I have upset anyone, I apologize. Most of all, I tried to be honest.

I hope in a long-winded way to have shone a light on a complicated relationship and industry.

Thank you so much for reading.

Glossary

American Paint: A breed of horse that combines the conformational characteristics of a western stock horse with the pinto spotting pattern of white and dark coat colours.

American Quarter Horse: A North American breed of horse that excels at sprinting short distances.

Appaloosa: A North American breed of horse with dark spots on a light background.

Appendix Quarter Horse: A first-generation cross between a Thoroughbred and an American Quarter Horse (or between registered and Appendix American Quarter Horses).

Arabian/Arab: One of the oldest breeds of horse. Originating on the Arabian Peninsula, it features a distinctive head shape and high tail carriage.

bascule: The round arc a horse's body naturally makes as it goes over a jump.

bay: Dark reddish-brown or brown body colour with black colouration on mane, tail, ear edges and lower legs.

Canadian horse: A solidly built, small but robust horse originating in Canada. Commonly dark coloured—black, bay or brown—with the occasional chestnut coat, but rarely grey.

caravans: Vehicles that are called travel trailers in North America.

Clydesdale: A heavy, powerful breed of draft horse originally bred in Scotland. Usually dark coloured with thick white hair on the lower legs.

colic: Abdominal pain caused by obstruction, gas or inflammation in the gut of a horse. Often fatal.

collection: Gathering a horse so it moves weight to its hindquarters, moving them under its body, raising its back and bringing its head down. This compresses the body of the horse and produces a shorter but more energetic stride.

conformation: The way in which a thing is formed; its shape or structure.

contact: Riding with a light but steady pressure between the rider's hands and the horse's mouth, with the reins in a straight line between hand and mouth.

cross ties: Ropes, attached to a wall or post on either side of a horse, that can be attached to the halter to keep the horse centred in the space where someone is grooming, tacking up or otherwise working with them.

dapple grey: Grey or white with darker spots.

dock: Cut the tail and tail bone of a horse short.

dressage: The training of a horse in obedience and deportment, especially for competition.

dun: Dull greyish-brown body colour, usually with a dorsal stripe (a stripe of a darker colour that runs along the spine).

equitation: The art and practice of horsemanship and horseback riding.

eventing: Also known as horse trials. An equestrian event where horse and rider compete against other competitors in three disciplines: dressage, cross-country and show jumping. Eventing can be a one-day or multi-day event.

Exmoor pony: Also known as a Celtic pony. A horse breed native to the British Isles, found roaming on the moors in southwest England. Well-adapted for cold weather: strong, hardy and noted for endurance.

extension: The opposite of collection. Lengthening the horse's stride without increasing the tempo of its movements, while keeping the horse balanced.

farrier: A professional who trims and shoes horses' hooves.

field hunter: A horse that is ridden for fox hunting.

flatwork: Exercises for a horse that don't require jumping. They are usually dressage exercises, like circles, turns and gait transitions.

flying changes: Movement a horse makes to change from one canter lead to the other.

Friesian horse: An all-black breed developed in the Netherlands. One of the only indigenous horses existing in that country and known for its large size, fast movement and smooth, elegant gaits.

gelding: A castrated male horse.

gymkhana: An equestrian event consisting of speed pattern racing and timed games for riders on horseback.

hacking: Also known as pleasure riding or trail riding. Riding for fun and enjoyment without any element of competition.

Haflinger: A breed of horse developed in Austria and northern Italy. Haflingers tend to be small (between 13.2 and 15 hands) and are always chestnut with flaxen mane and tail. They are used for riding and light draft work.

half-pass: A dressage movement in canter or trot where the horse moves sideways while moving forward.

hand: The unit of measure of a horse's height, equal to 4 inches (10.16 cm).

head collars: British name for halters, the headpiece made of leather, nylon, rope, etc., that is used to lead or tie up horses or other livestock.

herd bound: A horse that does not feel safe leaving the herd.

lateral work: Movements like leg yields or half-passes where the horse moves sideways and forward instead of just forward.

lunge line/lunging: A long rope on which a horse is held and made to move in a circle around its trainer. Lunging is often used to warm up a horse or burn off some energy, as well as for training.

mucking out: Cleaning a stall by taking out dirty straw or bedding and poop and spreading in new bedding. You can also muck out a pasture by picking up the poop.

nappy horse: A horse that will not move freely forward in the direction that you require. Once they have stopped at a given point, they may run backward, spin round or even rear.

on the bit: When a horse accepts contact with the rider's hands through the reins.

passage: A measured, collected, elevated and very cadenced trot in upper-level dressage.

Pelham bit: A bit with shanks and a curb chain. The shanks, which extend out of the horse's mouth on either side of the bit, act as a lever to increase the pressure when the rider pulls on the reins. The curb chain, which goes under the horse's chin, makes sure the bit doesn't rotate too far and also puts additional pressure on the mouth.

Percheron: A breed of heavy draft horse combining strength with agility and speed, originally bred in northern France.

piaffe: Move, especially on the spot, with a high, slow, trotting step.

piebald: Having irregular patches of two colours, especially black and white.

Prix St. Georges (PSG): The first level of international dressage as governed by the Fédération Equestre Internationale.

rig: A male horse with one or two testicles that are not visible (so it appears to be a gelding), but that are still producing testosterone, giving the horse a studdish temperament.

ringbone: The bony overgrowth (exostosis) that develops on or around the pastern bones in the wake of injury and/or inflammation. The overgrowth can be articular—affecting the joint—or develop on the side of a pastern bone, often where the ligaments attach.

round pen: A pen about forty-five feet in diameter encircled by a fence, about six or seven feet high, that allows you to work with a horse at liberty (without a rope or reins).

Shadbelly: Type of riding coat worn in certain equestrian situations by fox hunters, dressage riders, eventers (in the dressage phase of the higher levels) and, occasionally, other hunt seat riders.

Shetland pony: A small, hardy, rough-coated breed of pony.

short-coupled: A horse whose back is relatively short compared with the rest of their conformation.

spooky: A horse that is easily frightened or startled.

stud: A stallion; also a breeding farm, where stallions and mares are brought together.

Thoroughbred: A racehorse of a breed originating from the off-spring of English mares and Arab stallions, whose ancestry for several generations is fully documented.

through: In dressage, this means connecting your horse so impulsion from the hindquarters pushes through the body to the front end, lifting the back, dropping the head and collecting energy for the required movements.

torches: British word for flashlights.

Trakehner: A light warmblood breed of horse, originally developed at the East Prussian state stud farm in the town of Trakehner, from which the breed takes its name.

warmblood: A horse of any of various breeds having a middle-weight build and mild temperament, originally developed by crossing draft horses with Arabians or Thoroughbreds, and often used for dressage and jumping.

Welsh cob: A horse breed originating in Wales. They are known for their good temperament, hardiness and free-moving gaits. A cob is generally a draft-type pony traditionally used for pulling carts.

Wobblers: Also known as cervical vertebral malformation (CVM), a narrowing of the spinal canal as a result of vertebral malformations that can affect a horse's neurologic and musculoskeletal systems and lead to spasticity, ataxia and lack of coordination.

Mum and me.

Acknowledgements

Thank you for reading this book. I know that I have been extraordinarily lucky to be in the position to own one horse, let alone the many I've known in my life. Many people who are as horse crazy as I am never get that opportunity, so I understand and I am grateful. I want to thank all the gifted horse people and friends who helped me over the years. I had many great conversations with people while writing this book, and they helped shape it and allowed me to see things more clearly.

Thanks to my son, my sis, my fam, my ex-husband, Aunt Daphne, Hannah Peach, Lisa Fox, Lisa Davies, Sandown Chase Pony Club, Jabette Bullin Scott, Arlene Bynon, Jacqueline Brooks, Dianne O'Brien, Justin Hess, Jim Young, Elizabeth Gillis, Alley Dean, Jamie Kellock, Andria, Patty Ewuschuck, Berty Boyd, Marie Caloz and Baker's Saddlery.

My late dad, king of Redonda.

Kim Izzo, Carol McConnell, Elizabeth Jun'en Allen and Elizabeth Gillis for editing and correcting my terrible grammar and enabling me to get a *book deal*—who would have thought? Maybe things are working out. ☺

Natalie Howard

About the Author

Tamara Williamson is a new voice in Canadian literature. She is better known as a songwriter and has been performing and recording music for more than thirty-five years. Born and raised in London, England, she moved to Canada in 1991, where she was signed to BMG with her band Mrs. Torrance. She went on to an accomplished solo career and has released seven albums under her own name.

She has been described as an atmosphere builder, storyteller and provocateur. As a musician, Tamara takes the audience on a journey that keeps them hanging on each word or note. Her style was built at the forefront of grunge in the nineties, and she was dubbed the Godmother of Indie on Queen Street in Toronto. Always pushing her horizons, in 2019 Tamara received the Adams Award for her book/musical *The Break-Up Diet*, a ninety-minute alternative musical production that received five-star reviews at the Toronto Fringe Festival.

Tamara is also a lifelong horse enthusiast and dressage instructor. She has a successful company called Kurboom, which designs musical freestyles.

She lives in Uxbridge, Ontario, with her son, Angus.